BEING THE BEST

Whatever you can do, or dream you can, begin it! Boldness has genius, magic and power in it. Begin it now.

JOHANN WOLFGANG VON GOETHE

  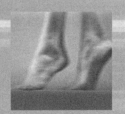 

BEING THE BEST

THE A-Z OF PERSONAL EXCELLENCE

NICHOLAS BATE

CAPSTONE

First published 2003 by
Capstone Publishing Limited (A Wiley Company)
The Atrium, Southern Gate, Chichester,
West Sussex PO19 8SQ, United Kingdom
e-mail: info@wiley-capstone.co.uk
www.capstoneideas.com

CIP catalogue records for this book are available from the British Library and the US Library of Congress

ISBN 1-84112-521-0

Designed and typeset by Baseline, Oxford, UK
Printed and bound by T.J. International Ltd, Padstow, Cornwall
This book is printed on acid-free paper

Substantial discounts on bulk quantities of Capstone books are available to corporations, professional associations and other organisations.

Please contact Capstone for more details on +44 (0)1865 798 623 or (fax) +44 (0)1865 240 941
or (e-mail) info@wiley-capstone.co.uk

Contents

Introduction

My own story is the origin of this book; there came a time when I had to admit my life was a mess.

Not at first glance. My job was prestigious and well paid. It gave security and a comfortable lifestyle. It was stimulating and very enjoyable. Initially.

The reality, however, was increasingly different. I was beginning to struggle. The ways of working which I had utilized in more junior roles were not working in my new, more senior roles, and the new world of working with instant communication and "just in time" processes seemed to be stretching me beyond my capability.

The signs were small, at the beginning: working longer hours, working at harder rates and without proper breaks. Then came the discovery that I didn't have the time to do what I wanted, particularly outside work. Then more significant signs: becoming unwell, not enjoying work and life becoming very one-dimensional.

Finally, the major signs. Something has to go; it always does. For some it's a relationship. For others it's their work. For me it was my health. Following months in intensive care, paralyzed by Guillaine-Barré syndrome (Joseph Heller, author of *Catch 22*, who also suffered and wrote a book about the experience, said anything named after two French doctors had to be really bad) and my eventual recovery, I decided things needed to change. I needed to run my life in a very different way.

But where to look for help? This was a challenge because so many of my colleagues and friends seemed to be suffering in similar ways: symptoms of ill health leading to a realisation that their lifestyle was not an ideal one. A scientist friend collapsed on a busy high street. A journalist friend began to suffer from food intolerances.

So I went back to basics and did some research. I looked for people who were getting the results, the version of success, that I was looking for. My definition of success: success that would release my potential with balance and enjoyment.

The changes I needed to make didn't seem obvious at first. But as I did my research, I eventually learned that there were straightforward strategies that would enable me to get the success I wanted. This, after all didn't seem too much to seek: a certain level of financial independence, an enjoyable job. Time for my family. Time for myself. And a feeling of purpose to it all.

As I continued conversations with others, I realised that I was not at all unique in my wishes. So many people were suffering overload, ill health and damaged relationships. Increasingly I realised that it didn't have to be that way.

Those statements probably sound very current. In fact, that was all a decade and a half ago! What I went through then is now all too common and becoming increasingly so; success can come at great cost. But it need not: Being the Best is straightforward and accessible if you know the principles.

The consultancy that I formed in 1988, Strategic Edge, still has the same vision: to enable individuals to realise and release their potential. And that's what this book will do for you.

This book is about "Being the Best". More completely: Being the Best you can be by identifying your niche. It'll encourage you to take your natural genetic advantages and realise and release your full potential. It'll enable you to be truly successful; to reach your vision with balance. Based on my own original researches of fifteen years ago, it has developed since then through constantly working with those who are striving to be the best.

It has always been a goal of mine when teaching and coaching individuals to help them absorb ideas and concepts as quickly and as easily as possible; that's how the A to Z structure came about. The A to Z of personal success summarizes the twenty-six characteristics that allowed those who become the best in their field to do so. The A to Z is based solely on working with practitioners. There is a minimum of theory.

To help you further each letter, each characteristic – bar two – has at least one mini case study. Every one of these case studies is based on a real situation which I have dealt with in a workshop or during coaching. Deciding which studies to choose was hard; in over fifteen years of coaching and running workshops I have worked with thousands of people. In the end I have chosen ones which I feel are both representative and illustrate a particular characteristic. Clearly I have changed names and details where appropriate.

My role in writing this book is to act as a catalyst. I do not have all the answers: beware of those who say they do! However I do believe (and I feel my work to date bears this out) that there are timeless principles from which we can all benefit.

How might you use the A to Z? Here are some suggestions:
- Focus on a different letter each day of the month.

- Choose a letter which appeals and focus on it until you feel you are living and breathing the principle.

- Should you set up a learning team, get different members of the team to work on different aspects.

Above all, start giving attention to the characteristics which you seek. There are principles encapsulated in the A to Z which we break at our peril.

Being the Best in your chosen niche is not necessarily easy, but it is certainly a lot more attractive, a lot more fun, and a lot more enlivening compared to the other options...

...Enjoy the book.
Enjoy your life.

A is Attention

Attention

A IS ATTENTION. It's where the art of being successful starts; all twenty-five other characteristics are dependent upon this one. To be successful at something, to be able to say "yes, I achieved that" or "yes, I can do that now" or "finally, I'm on the path which I wanted" we must give it – whatever we want – attention. Attention means we give our desire, our goal, three types of focus: appropriate dedicated time, appropriate dedicated energy and appropriate dedicated mindset. Without the consistent application of these three factors we are unlikely to achieve our goal; success will not be ours.

Isn't it a fairly obvious point? Well, not necessarily. In this increasingly busy world we have become very good at thinking and talking about changes we wish to make. But there is a difference – a big difference – between thinking and talking and actually doing. The danger is that as we think and talk we often feel we are doing. And as we talk more and more about losing weight, or writing our book, or learning that language, or gaining promotion and yet nothing changes we begin to feel disillusioned: why are we not getting what we want? We complain that we have been "working on this for so long". Not true. But with sufficient attention, we will get the change we want.

For example, have you talked about:
- making a million,
- losing some weight,
- getting out more,
- writing a book,
- doing an MBA,
- watching more foreign films,
- learning yoga,
- sorting out your finances,
- getting up earlier,

or simply doing anything different to your current routine, and then noticed that nothing happened?

That's what we want to change. We want to ensure that our intellectual wish becomes our physical reality. Remember: think is not walk. Neither is talk. Give real attention and gain real results: maybe not instantly, maybe not as easily as you would like. But it will happen.

So, the three factors are: appropriate dedicated time, appropriate dedicated energy and appropriate dedicated mindset. What do "appropriate" and "dedicated" mean? By appropriate level, we mean sufficient time, or energy or mindset to raise this issue into our everyday consciousness: it's literally "on our mind". By dedicated we mean you allow nothing to come in its way. You may have noticed that there are only a few things each day upon which you can truly focus. These are the things which are in your everyday conversation or, more colloquially, in your face. Make this goal one of them.

Appropriate Dedicated Time

Factor one in developing, improving and achieving what you want is to shift from occasional mental attention on the skill or topic (i.e., an almost random thought about a change you might like) to maximizing mental (i.e., keep thinking about it until it's happening) and physical (i.e., keep doing it until it works) attention. This of course requires that you dedicate time. Follow this procedure.

1. Decide clearly what it is that you want. For the moment we are going to assume that you know. Perhaps you don't. Or you are a little vague or concerned that your idea seems too simplistic or naive. Whatever, when we look at C for Compass, you'll know what to do. So we will assume you do for the moment.

2. Open your diary: paper or electronic. It is going to get a new use. No longer is it just for recording appointments and occasionally listing "stuff to be done". It's now a planning tool, too, for getting things to happen. Mark when and for how long you are going to dedicate time to this change that you want. Make it a block of time – not just a point of time. For instance, write "10–3, Saturday, watercolours" not "10, Sat, watercolours". Blocks of time dedicate the time to a cause. Points of time have a habit of merging with other points of time.

3. Whatever happens, stick to that time. If you do have to cancel a time, make a new time. And keep doing this if necessary. You are wiring your body to be accepting of change and that you will get what you want eventually. This latter point is critical. Don't give up. Be persistent. Be attentive.

Remember that you can always find time for what is important. But you need to make it important to you. If something which is important is not getting done then you will need to change your priorities. Remember that time is easily sucked away. On average, adults in Europe watch 3.5 hours of television per day. Do you really need all of that TV? Don't whinge when you can't get the time for your gardening, writing, reading in the large chunks you would wish; simply take what you can. Maybe it is the case that you can't get half-days for your writing; do it in one-hour chunks instead. Or maybe you can never get enough time to travel to anywhere interesting to develop your photographic skills. So take your camera shopping and practice on something ordinary.

Appropriate Dedicated Mindset

Factor two is your mindset. Approach the change or goal with an absolutely determined mindset. Don't allow anything to come in the way. Be accepting of natural, limiting mindsets such as "this is going to be hard". Yes, it might, but that needn't stop you. Be aware that the way you are thinking will have subtle and not-so-subtle effects on the results that you get; the personal psychology of how you approach this goal will probably be the biggest of the three factors. We will do a lot more work on this when we look at B for Beliefs. As an introduction think about how you will react if your plans don't work out initially. Will you see it as failure? Or as feedback to try a different approach? Will you insist on having half-days for your writing or will you try and work with just 90 minutes? Notice how your mindset affects the way you behave.

Appropriate Dedicated Energy

Factor three is your energy. Put some oomph behind your project. Now decide actually to do something in those times which you have scheduled. Go for that walk, work on your MBA, do whatever you have promised yourself that you will do. Energy builds. Once you start you will get improved results. See Compass Point 2 – mind/body (in C for Compass) for more on building energy. I often work with individuals who liaise internationally in global markets. A common goal such individuals would like to realise is language development. Here's such an example.

David's career was simply not going to progress until he acquired fluency in everyday business Japanese. He had of course known that for years; he spent about 30 percent of his time in Japan on behalf of his UK parent organization. But he had got nowhere. He'd used tape sets, grammar texts. He had received coaching at home and in Japan. There was very little to show for it.

But now he was up against it; his last review had stated in writing that unless he got to a respectable level in Japanese within the year his company would need to replace him with a local specialist. That coincided with an interesting dinner party conversation where David had expressed a worry that he just wasn't a linguist. "Not necessarily true," the woman next to him replied, "you simply aren't giving it enough attention."

It rang true for David, so he went for it.

Dedicated time. He scheduled 45 minutes every day. Everything else which could go, did go. Whether he felt like it or not, he worked alternate days on grammar and vocabulary. And as he made progress most days, he actually began to enjoy it. Previously he had fitted it in when he could, which was never.

Dedicated mindset. He got really focused on making this work. And he got really focused on what would happen if it didn't work. Previously he had tackled his language work with increasing resentment.

Dedicated energy. He made sure he worked on it every morning, his best time. Previously it had tended to be the end of the day in hotel rooms.
Nine months later David had it cracked. He was regularly congratulated on the standard of his Japanese.

80 percent of success is turning up.
WOODY ALLEN

Let's now take some other specific examples.

So you want to get fit?
1. Give it appropriate time. Decide the level of fitness you would like. If in any doubt at all start at the level of walking and taking the stairs. Open your diary (paper or electronic): mark in five

20-minute chunks; do make sure that they are blocks of time. If you can't do anything this week, then do it the following week. Make it happen.

2. Give it appropriate mindset. Be aware that other people get fit, even after years of inactivity, so that there is no reason why you can't do the same.

3. Give it appropriate energy. This one could be circular! Start small. Have a good night's sleep, get up and take that exercise. Notice how much better you sleep the following night.

So you want to write a book?

1. Give it appropriate time. Every day write three pages. At this stage don't worry too much about the quality, simply get used to writing. Once you have become a writer, then you can write a book.

2. Have an appropriate mindset. Don't worry about whether it will get published, don't worry about whether anyone will think it is good. Simply concentrate on a) becoming a writer, and b) writing the book.

3. Give it appropriate energy. Choose the best time of day for you and reserve it for your writing.

So you want to get promoted?
I suspect you're getting the hang of this now!

1. *Time:* set up four conversations with people who can help.

2. *Mindset:* "I'm now ready for the next stage" not "I wonder if..."

3. *Energy:* warm up before conversations.

B is Belief

Belief

Learn the following mantra; it may be all you need to know to ensure that you are consistently successful. *Your beliefs create your behaviours which create your results.* **Understand this point and you have the fast-track route to whatever you wish to achieve.**

Beliefs are our software; they dictate our actions. Take the business of being assertive. You can go on all the assertiveness training available to you but if you don't believe that you have a right to be assertive with, say, your manager, guess what? You'll remain passive. And the poor results that you get will certainly reinforce your initial belief of "there's no point in being assertive; my manager always wins these discussions". To be assertive – or to develop any skill – we need to work on our beliefs first.

In the business world, we are surprisingly late in coming to capitalize on the psychology of our effectiveness. Now let's get a little more clarity. There are two kinds of beliefs.

Firstly, empowering beliefs. Empowering beliefs help and support us. An excellent example would be "there is no failure, only feedback". Things don't always go to plan. The presentation is a mess, the business plan is rejected, the person you love doesn't love you, you've been made redundant (hopefully not all in one day). How do you stay resourceful, how do you move on in such situations? By realising that it is an opportunity to learn, grow and develop. It is feedback, not failure. That is in no way to trivialize what has occurred to you and it doesn't preclude a period of sadness or "fed-up-ness". But those states are intended to be brief only, so move on and learn. Nor does this belief condone a cock-up nor suggest that you put in anything less than 100 percent to achieve a goal. What it is saying, is given that something hasn't worked out as you would like, what can you do, what can you get from it?

Secondly, limiting beliefs. A limiting belief holds us back. A limiting belief can disable us, such as "I have a poor memory" or "I'll never make a good consultant." If that's your belief, that's how you will act, that's what you'll notice and that's the behaviour that will be reinforced: it is the low expectation we have of ourselves. And yet when people come on my seminars they find they do not have problems with assertiveness, or coaching or remembering names, because we have tackled and removed the limiting belief behind the behaviour.

A brief word about "real beliefs". Individuals will often ask: "Surely there are some real limitations?" Of course, and it is well worth heeding these for good practical safety reasons! Thus, don't jump off tall buildings unaided and expect to survive. But that's not really the point. The point is that our own mental limitations are so much lower than our physical limitations. Mentally we have effectively reduced our physical capability. We can invariably step-up several times and find that it works.

I am convinced that the most frequent area for creating rapid breakthrough is when individuals are able to transform their belief sets. Here's a recent example.

Pierre was a talented guy, but he often seemed too "nice" or too "soft" for corporate life. He tended to build his career in an organization to a certain point, but would then meet the tougher people who often lurk in the higher echelons.

He would find contact with them uncomfortable. To avoid conflict he would take the easy way out and resign. In times of growth he was a good catch and anyway he increased his salary considerably with each move. Initially those near Pierre saw this as evidence of his ambition. Pierre himself began to recognize that it wasn't a strategy, it was an escape from conflict.

A breakthrough came for Pierre when once again he began to sense in himself a desire to move on, but realised at the same time that he loved this current job and that it would be crazy to leave. And just as he was dealing with that turmoil he found himself (reluctantly) booked on a two-day assertiveness course.

Within the first hour Pierre had changed his complete outlook and realised where he was going wrong; he simply wasn't defending his own rights.

He became an avid learner and realised that he had a limiting belief about what it was OK for him to say in meetings. He practiced his assertiveness skills in simple, low-risk situations and then became adept at it. His belief changed. He saw conflict for what it was: a different perspective. He began to enjoy asking fair, respectful questions which would turn conflict into positive actions.

Eighteen months later Pierre hadn't moved on. In fact he was now part of the executive team.

If you think you can, you can. If you think you can't, you can't.
HENRY FORD.

How best do we use this information to enable us to become more successful? Firstly, by focusing on empowering beliefs. Secondly, by editing our limiting beliefs. Remember our mantra. A belief drives a behaviour which will get a certain result. If we want results which allow us to be successful, what beliefs do we need? Here are seven such empowering beliefs.

1. I can

This is the self-directing belief. This is the belief which reminds us that we can improve, we can tackle anything. The flip side, I can't, needs to be recognized for what it really is: I choose not to. Once you realise that, you can choose to do things.

Thus "I can't become a good presenter" is a limiting belief. You surely can stand up in front of people, you can learn how to take questions, you can... Yes, it may take some time. But you can.

2. There is no failure, only feedback

This is the learning belief. Everything that happens to you is a highly customized, highly focused personal development program. Such training might normally be infrequent and possibly very expensive. Here it is, whenever you need it and at no extra cost! Use it!

Thus: you didn't get the promotion you were looking for. OK; why not? What could you do differently in the future? Stay resourceful. There is no reason why it need be seen as failure, but every reason why it might be seen as feedback.

3. I make the real world

This is the belief of perception. You can decide how to look at things. Many people won't make certain changes because they believe that such changes simply will not work for them "in the real world". What do they mean by that? They simply mean it's not necessarily everyone else's perception. True. But it doesn't stop it being *your* perception.

On my seminars it is simply a matter of time before someone says, "But Nick, what about the real world?" or "Wouldn't you agree that in the real world..." The simple answer is that the real world is what you make of it.

Thus, wouldn't you agree that not every one wants to work in a "win–win" way? True. Or that not everyone is interested in their personal development? True. But don't let that stop you. You can still get the huge benefits.

4. I choose

This is the decision-making belief. "I choose" recognizes that the more we practice choosing, the more we open up a range of new behaviours. When something happens to us do we respond in our usual conditioned way, or do we choose a new way forward?

We easily become conditioned, as with Pavlov's famous dogs. But we can choose to break that conditioning. Start with easy examples. How about changing your route to work? There is a better route, simply look for it.

5. There's a reason for this person's behaviour.

This is the empathy belief. This is the belief which says "I know this person isn't behaving as I would like. I would have preferred it if they had been quieter, friendlier, more dynamic or whatever. But given that they are like this, how can I best work with them?" We'll consider more on this subject when we look at emotional intelligence, often known as EQ. People are different. Skin colour, sex, age... all the way through to the deepest levels of thinking.

6. What does this say about me?

This is a particularly powerful learning belief. When something hasn't gone or isn't going as you would wish, particularly when you are working with another person, rather than allocating 100 percent of the blame to the other person or the situation, think, "What does it say about me?" Because then you will be contributing to the challenge, even if it's only 0.05 percent.

If you resent someone because they don't seem to be a great listener, just stop for a moment and reflect on your own listening skills.

7. There's always a way

This belief will help you with challenges. Notice how much you have overcome so far in your life and how much you can still overcome. So you really, really want that job in marketing? You know you can get it if you have this belief and you give it sufficient attention.

Use all these beliefs as your new software.

But what do we do about limiting beliefs? One strategy is to reverse the process by which they were created. A limiting belief is normally created through limited evidence which we take as definitive evidence. We then generalize from that limited evidence.

Thus "I'm no good at drawing" perhaps comes from:
■ Unhelpful advice when at school. ("You'll never be an artist, will you?")
■ Internalizing that advice as a belief. ("I guess I'm no good at drawing, then.")
■ Continuing to notice only that evidence which reinforces it. ("Hmm – my drawing doesn't look much like a real landscape.")

To break that limiting belief:
1. Be aware. Develop self-awareness. This allows you to notice your behaviours. And as you do, you can adjust them. Simple strategies for developing self-awareness are take time out, seek 360-degree feedback, read development books such as this one.
2. Deliberately break that limiting belief in an easy way. Practice mind mapping for instance, using pictures to develop your drawing or speak out in meetings to practice your assertiveness.
3. Notice your self-confidence developing, which becomes self-fulfilling.
4. Notice your success. Allow your approach to be individualistic. Set high standards, but don't try and be someone else.
5. Simply be the best version you can of yourself.

Running has always been more of a mental problem than a physical problem to me.
ROGER BANNISTER

C is Compass

Compass

No doubt you use the words "important" and "urgent": perhaps at work, no doubt at home, perhaps in a discussion in the pub. You may however, have never stopped to consider the real meaning of these two terms. Things which are important are things which will help you meet your goals; things which are urgent are those which need to be done now. Thus if you are regularly going to the gym then this is an important activity as it supports your goal of being fit. If you have a warning letter from the bank about your unauthorized overdraft, then clearly it is time-bound, it is urgent, it needs addressing.

Firstly, realise that urgent does not necessarily equal important. Yes, these emails do need a response (they have been sitting in your inbox for a couple of days). They are urgent. But in the big picture, what has happened? They are distracting you from something which is actually critically important: completing the sales plan which you are trying to write for the next financial year, just a couple of months away, and which may well dictate the success of the organization in the year to date.

Secondly, the interaction of these two parameters – important and urgent – creates two types of time. One which is important and urgent; this is clock time. It is driven by the watch and clock, by external factors. In this part of time you will generally be reactive: the customer call ("Why is our server down?"), the home crisis ("Little Jim has fallen off the swings and wants you here!"). There is also a piece of time which is important and non-urgent. This is compass time. You choose specifically to do actions in this piece of time; you choose your direction. You are proactive. Unfortunately non-urgent can sound non-worthwhile. Far from it. Consider that in important and urgent time we will find topics such as customer responsiveness issues and crises; however, in important and non-urgent we will find topics such as planning, health, relationships, financial planning, strategy and, of course, personal development and training. These are vitally (literally) important. But true, they don't need to be done today, or tomorrow or perhaps even next week. A much better term than important and non-urgent is important and investing. That's what these topics really are. They are investing for the future.

Actions in clock time will always tend to happen because of pressure created by adrenaline and fear: we will sort out the customer problem because we can see the immediate consequences if we don't address it.

Compass time, though, requires us to be proactive. And it is lack of proactivity that is the downfall of many individuals and, for that matter, organizations. However, for those of us who want to be truly successful, it's an important area to which to give attention. When we are proactive we address the issues which will help us in the future, and which are much easier to address when they are not urgent.

LifeCompass℠ is a Strategic Edge tool for getting back on track, for being proactive, for addressing that which is important and investing. There are six compass points.

Compass Point 1 – career
Decide to manage your career; no one else will. You may be fortunate and have a supportive employer or manager. You may have a mentor. But no one will be able to give it the same level of tender, loving care as you. Start today.

Invest in your skills; become a lifelong learner. I will be giving you lots of tips on how to do that. In particular, see L for Lifelong Learning.

Regularly ask yourself the questions "Where do I want to be in three years time?" and "How can I get there?" Put aside your limiting beliefs (review B for Beliefs). Give it attention and it will happen. Each month decide which are the actions you need to take to ensure that you are on track.

In summary: don't put up with your job or career, certainly don't dumb down your life. Develop your career so that it is enjoyable. Invest in yourself so that you are marketable and highly employable. Remember, this is a world of low predictability, high uncertainty, rapid change. Decide to be something which you truly enjoy and are good at. There's considerably more help on this topic in N for Niche.

Compass Point 2 – mind/body

Read this several times: this mind/body is all I have got!

Whatever you do will be dependent upon the quality of your thinking and your energy; in other words, upon your state. Given that, it is surprising how poorly many of us look after it. Let me give you a simple methodology which those who are best in their niche follow, summarized as MEDS.

Meditation. They take time out. It may simply be early morning reflection in their study. It may be going for a walk, or it may be a more formal meditation.

Exercise. Our body is designed for regular cardio-vascular activity. That is part of its maintenance procedure. Walk every day. Take the stairs. Swim. Bicycle. Build up slowly. Get fitter and fitter.

Diet. Fuel in, results out. Just do the simplest of things: drink sufficient water. Take oxygen breaks, walk, stretch. Focus more on eating complex carbohydrates rather than simple sugars.

Sleep. A significant limiting belief that many have is that they can do without sleep, perhaps because they have heard that is what true leaders and real heroes can do. But this is a myth. Clear your sleep debt and get sufficient sleep every night.

Compass Point 3 – finance

Manage your finances. Regularly rate them from one to ten. Ten is when they are in outstanding order: in particular when you know your financial independence day, the day you no longer need to work to earn money. It is a date you are happy with. Zero is when your finances are in a dreadful state; regularly overdrawn, no long-term savings. Whatever the rating you have given yourself, resolve to improve it.

Poorly resolved finances are debilitating. They distract us. Don't chase money for happiness or standard of living. Focus on your quality of life; your happiness will come through that. Read that again and allow the point to really sink in: there is a distinct difference between quality of life and standard of living. Chase the latter and you may find the former plummets. Chase the former and you'll get what you want.

I have found that the concept of LifeCompass[SM] helps clarify thinking.

When Sally joined the bank as a graduate trainee her main motivation was simply to earn as much money as she could in order to clear her very large student debts. Unfortunately she disliked the work so much that she ended up adding to her debts as she compensated for the dull days by partying and going out.

Eventually she had a highly embarrassing ticking off from her manager about the state of her personal finances, which was now affecting her work. She was shocked into looking at her life as a whole, using the interconnecting compass points of LifeCompass^{SM}, and realised that "Finance" would be unlikely to be resolved until she was honest with herself about "Career".

She was bold. She got herself a much lower paid job in a theatre (her love) with two evenings a week working in a restaurant where her new-found enthusiasm for life ensured she gained good tips. She didn't feel the need to go out as much and quickly got to a state where her outgoings were at last lower than her income.

Sally will still need another year to clear her debts, but one year after leaving the bank she has gained promotion at the theatre and written a simple budget guide to organic cooking for students.

Things happen when you set your LifeCompass^{SM}.

Compass Point 4 – relationships

They bring joy, they bring anxiety and everything in between. Work on the five As of relationships.

Give them *Attention:* a relationship is organic. It needs looking after; spend time developing it: your partner, your child, your team.

Be *Aware* of difference: it's not a pain nor a nuisance. In both business and personal relationships it's the spark which makes a relationship work.

Appreciate: catch people doing things right.

Always have time for *Affection* in your most personal of relationships.

Act first in improving any relationship.

Compass Point 5 – fun

What is the point if you are not having fun? Decide what would be fun for you. Put aside the limiting belief that "I'm too old/at too tricky a stage in my career/whatever to have fun." Fun is vital; it leads to passion for life. Whatever you do, do it with passion. Fun is healing. Think about your kind of fun: have romance, have adventure. Go beyond defining fun as getting drunk. Link to the other compass points. Fun is enjoying your work. Fun is being healthy. Fun is contributing.

Compass Point 6 – contribution

What's your place in the bigger picture? Think team, community, environment, society. In what small ways could you help? Place your vote! Recycle a little more. Identify and support a charity.

Not only will it help the charity or organization you decide to support, it will help your personal evolution.

The compass points help people who have it all realise what components they are missing.

Juan was a very intelligent, multi-lingual lawyer. Aggressive and ambitious, by the age of thirty four he had apartments in London, Paris and Madrid. And the best in everything; from cars to kitchens, from suits to saunas. But he had a terrible feeling of "been there, done that". He got his buzz from women and alcohol. And his marriage was breaking up.

LifeCompass[SM] thinking encouraged Juan to downgrade to just three day's law work per week. He settled in Paris. He rebuilt his relationships. He started some voluntary work. And he came alive. At last.

LifeCompass[SM] is about authenticity.

Follow your bliss. – JOSEPH CAMPBELL

To keep your LifeCompass[SM] alive:
- Regularly review it: once a month is ideal.
- If you are in a close relationship, share your findings and support each other's goals.
- Note the actions from your compass on your Master List (see O for Organized).

To be successful, ensure that you act more from your compass and less from the clock.

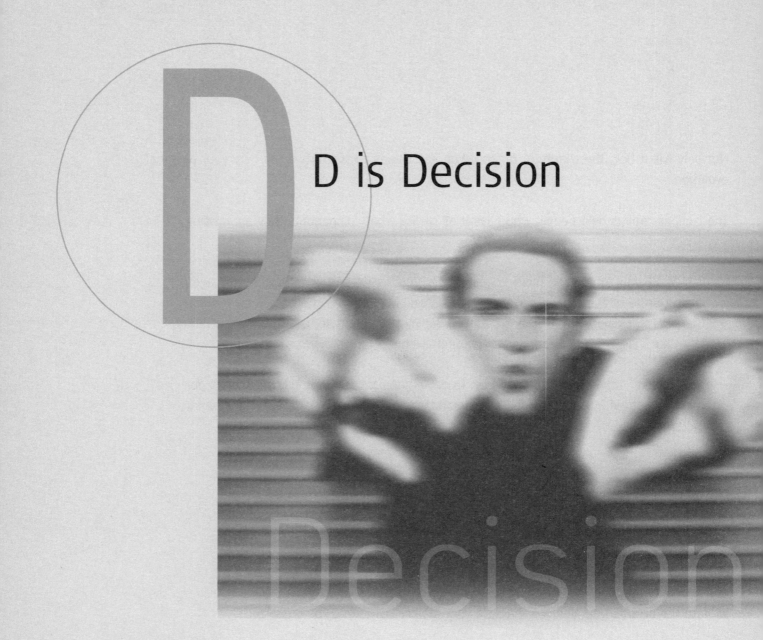

D is Decision

Decision

To become successful we will need to make some decisions; a decision to do something, a decision to change something. Maybe simply to put aside some time for reflection, maybe a small decision, maybe a big decision, maybe a radical decision. But you will definitely need to make some decisions. Giving attention is excellent. Working on your beliefs, vital. Setting your compass, critical. But it is when you take decisions that you begin to get the results.

Obvious point? Perhaps. After all, many feel that they do make decisions, but despite that, they feel frustrated that nothing seems to change: they decided to get fit this year, they decided to read more to their children, they decided to ask for a pay rise. But nothing happened. Here's the fundamental point which needs to be understood and which we will explore in detail in the subsequent paragraphs. And it is this: a decision is not a true decision unless we take an immediate action. We must move from an intellectual or ordinary change to a practical, radical change.

There are five important stages to a decision. You do not necessarily need to do all of them in detail, but you do need to consider them.

Stage 1

This is a stage of awareness. An awareness creeps up on us (sometimes, of course, it hits us like a bolt from the blue) that a decision needs to be made. Clearly, this will be through some kind of feedback. Some of this will be formal: sales figures have consistently dropped month by month; written feedback suggests that your technical briefings are not getting through to the customer. Or your friends say tell you that you haven't been looking that well recently. However, importantly, some feedback will be more qualitative; a gut feeling, a sense that things aren't right. Don't ignore this. Especially if you feel you are normally pretty "scientific" in your thinking. One paradox of much scientific thinking is that gut feeling starts the inspiration for a discovery which is later backed up by quantitative thinking. So decide to decide. Notice what's happening to you, how people react. This is Stage 1: being aware that a decision needs to be made. Don't put off this stage. The earlier you react to the feedback, to the feeling, the more easily you will be able to deal with it and create an elegant solution.

Having decided to give up smoking, Louise crumpled up her packet of cigarettes and chucked them away. She then calculated the amount of money she would normally have spent on cigarettes during the rest of the week and put that money in a charity box. Finally she emailed her MP to ask what his policy was on reducing smoking amongst young people and asked whether there was anything she could do to help.

That's momentum.

Stage 2

Stage 2 is how we make the decision. Make the decision with the help of a framework, something which pulls the factors together so that you can consider them more easily. A good framework has two components: a "bag" for all the data and a "weighing machine" for considering the pros and cons: the detail.

The simplest way to do this is to put pen to paper and draw two columns, the pros and the cons. Fill each column with as many points as you can identify. Then leave it for 24 hours.

Whichever route you use will help you balance the pros and cons of the decision that you need to make. This stage is about using your reflective intelligence. Our reflective intelligence supports our other two intelligences: our neural (that which we are born with) and our experiential (that which builds with experience). Our reflective intelligence works when we stop, and in this busy, pressurized, now, now, now world we do too little of that.

At the end of a bitter argument with his wife about work/life balance Harry had promised that he would arrange a weekend break for the two of them. He did so immediately.

He felt that their relationship had already started to mend because he was taking action.

Stage 3

This stage is when we make the decision. Before we discuss the structure of a great decision, let's just highlight a potential area of downfall. When many people take a mental decision (ones like "I will start saving" or "right, I will stop smoking") there is a sense of relief: "Thank goodness, I've got that out of the way." However it's vital to realise that no real progress has yet been made. So how about agreeing with yourself that a decision is only a decision once you have taken an immediate and specific action? After all it's only after the first saving deposit has been made or when you truly throw away your cigarettes for good that you can say you've carried out your decision.

So a decision is not a decision without an immediate action. There are three characteristics of a great action:

- Firstly, that it is measurable so that you know exactly when you have achieved it. "Save more" is not measurable. "Save £20 a month, every month" is measurable.
- Secondly, that you have time/date stamped it: "By October 1, I'll be saving £15 a month."
- Thirdly you should make it "brain and body friendly": easy to understand and easy to do.

These facts are often quoted and they are of course entirely logical. So why don't people do it? When individuals are very honest they reveal that one reason they are reluctant to set commitments is because they are anxious about potential failure. If I say that I'll be running for 30 minutes four times a week by February 1 and I'm not, then I've failed. If I don't set a date I haven't failed. True; but then I haven't progressed either! How about if we stop seeing it as a simple polarized view of success or non-success? How about a gradual scale of improvement onto which you can only get a place by starting? Remember that belief: no failure, only feedback (see B for Belief).

Having decided that he needed a heart-to-heart with his daughter's maths teacher about why the child's results were so poor, Tim jotted down all the reasons he wasn't happy with the situation as the basis for a letter.

Excellent: he was making progress already.

Stage 4

Stage 4 is optional. But don't underestimate its power. You now have a decision and you have a first action. But of course there will be subsequent decisions. And for some of the decisions that you make (starting a business, reinventing yourself) there may well be a wealth of interdependencies or resource decisions you need to make. You are now moving into the field of project management. All this means is that when we have made decisions on action, we decide when they will be done, who will do them and whether they are dependent upon anything else. Dependence is a subtle point; you may well have hoped to have had some work done in your house at some stage but everything has ground to a halt because a component for the boiler is missing. Everything was dependent upon that particular component. We refer to it as being on the critical path. The critical path through a project is the one on which there can be no delays otherwise the whole of the project will be delayed. Make sure you know what is on yours and, if necessary, learn how to use project management software to identify it.

Stage 5

To share or not to share your decision, that is the bigger question? So you decide to go it alone and start that business, or you do decide to go for that directorship or you decide to simplify and reduce your lifestyle drastically so one of you can be a full-time parent. Do you communicate this to the world? Only if you feel you will be supported. Remember, not everyone will support you in the changes that you wish to make (see I for Internally-referenced). A simple guideline is to share your goals with those whom you know will support you; do not share your goals with those you know will only try and weaken your resolve.

Start becoming more aware of the decisions you need to make. Tune into the signals which you will get from head and heart. Ensure you have enough time to reflect on those decisions. And then make those decisions with a clear action attached: ones that are measurable, timely and sufficiently brain-friendly to be actionable.

Whatever you can do, or dream you can, begin it! Boldness has genius, magic and power in it. Begin it now. – GOETHE

"It is when you take decisions that you begin to get the results."

E is Emotional Intelligence or EQ

Howard Gardener and Daniel Goleman have both done significant work in reminding us that intelligence does not simply come in one format. The one which we articulate so often is of course numerical/linguistic intelligence, often referred to as IQ. Gardener's studies and publications have shown the existence and importance of other types of intelligence, particularly emotional intelligence, often referred to as EQ. To be truly effective, to be truly successful we need to address both IQ and EQ. In fact Daniel Goleman states that EQ is twice as important as IQ.

Emotional Intelligence is considered to have five levels:

1. Self-awareness.

2. Self-regulation.

3. Self-motivation.

4. Empathy.

5. Interpersonal skills.

Let's take a look at each of these levels in turn.

Self-awareness

This is the first stage of developing excellent EQ. Self-awareness is the ability to notice one's own behaviours, feelings, reactions. Thus you are aware of yourself reading this; now notice how you can direct your awareness, perhaps to a sound outside.

And clearly, self-awareness must be the first stage in our evolving our EQ. Without self-awareness, how can we change our behaviour? With self-awareness we can realise we are getting angry in a meeting, we can realise we need to change our diet.

There are several routes.

■ **Meditation**.
In whatever form – taking time out, thinking, reflecting, walking. Stress drives us to act without reflection. This is useful in an emergency but not so useful in many personal and business situations. As we let go of stress we pull apart the stimulus and our response. We allow ourselves to use the gap between the two to adjust and perhaps change any inappropriate auto-response.

■ **MBTI or other psychometrics.**
Such tests – and always use recognized tests administered by qualified practitioners – give helpful insights into our behaviour, into such things as why maybe you have a craving for things to be "sorted out" (not everybody does!), or why you can't stand planning.

■ **Reading**.
Read anything outside your main subject area.

■ **Workshops**.
Again, use those given by quality practitioners who live and breathe their principles.

■ **360-degree feedback.**
Feedback, of course, has to be a route to self awareness. Many worry: as they say, "people are so poor at receiving feedback". I agree, but with feedback from several people you can begin to notice themes. And it's those themes which will help you.

Self-regulation

Once you are aware you can adjust. OK, so this person is irritating. Should I be irritated? What would be the best way forward? Self-regulation is perhaps another term for professionalism. A professional is someone who does what is necessary even when they don't feel like doing it.

Now, to self-regulate you will clearly need to make an effort. Certainly, to achieve what you want to achieve in order to be successful requires the correct level of attention. That we have already discussed in A for Attention. That attention must then be developed with the correct level of effort. But what is the correct level? We seem to polarize into the "success is easy" school and the "success is rare and hard to achieve" school.

"Success is easy"

Perhaps one unfortunate message of much personal development literature over the last 15 years has been that success is easy. This sound bite has, I believe, confused many and caused some to become disillusioned when their dreams have not apparently come to fruition. Yes, success is easy in the sense of what to do. It is easy in the sense that all one needs to do is start. And it can become easier as you start getting the results that you want. However it is important to realise that it can be hard in the sense of the effort needed to be put in, hard in the sense that not everyone is appreciative and supportive of your changes, hard in the sense that we can get lost on the way. But success will come if the effort is applied. Let's be absolutely clear. In changes you wish to make, in goals you wish to achieve, there will be many factors upon which you will depend.

But one will undoubtedly be that ***results obtained are proportional to effort put in***.

Initially these results often seen disproportionately low – a lot of effort is apparently needed to achieve very little. Then you'll notice that it becomes linear: results in equal results out. And then, amazingly, it takes off. As you put more effort in, you get staggering results out; they become disproportionately high.

"Success is rare and hard to achieve"
For people who believe this, success is never an expectation. Success is something that always comes to other people. Now, a whole range of facts will be causing this kind of thinking, many of which we have already looked at. Certainly limiting beliefs will be holding this type of person back. Certainly they won't have made a clear decision. But, importantly, they are not putting in the right kind effort. Their effort is short-term, get through the day, survival mode. It is not thinking longer term, not thinking "Where am I trying to get to?"

For people in this category, EQ will be harder to achieve.
Self-motivation
This clearly links with motivation. This is such an important topic we will look at it more fully and properly in M for Motivation. Let's just say here that motivation is not something to wait for.

Empathy
This is the ability to consider others; to understand their feelings, to relate to them. Practice empathy by asking the simple question: "If I were in their shoes, how would I be feeling?" Review the five As of relationships in Compass Point 4 (see C for Compass).

Interpersonal skills
This is our portfolio of skills which we can use. Many of these we will address through our study of the A to Z, such as assertiveness, quantum thinking and organization.

Emotional Intelligence will make the difference between someone being ordinarily effective and someone being outstandingly effective.

Simon was a great team leader. Technically he was second to none. His promotion was what he had always sought as recognition of his ability. After all, he spent time with each member of the team. He was clear and thorough with his one-on-one reviews; no point was ever overlooked. He checked milestones; he invested in their training.

But when 360-degree feedback time came Simon was shocked: "robotic approach," "clinical," "he's not interested in me, simply in project deadlines," "I told him I was pregnant and all he wanted to know was best delivery date," were typical of the accusations thrown at him.

Simon had yet to discover the power and joy of EQ. The great thing was that the feedback had broken a pattern and got him to think deeply about his self-awareness. His sensitivity built rapidly and he was keen to learn and to be a great leader.

One year later Simon's feedback was excellent. He was considered one of the most effective team leaders in the company. Simon's rapidly developing EQ coupled with his high technical competence made him highly employable.

Develop your EQ. The right balance of IQ and EQ is essential for excellence and essential for success.

F is Fear

Fear

What so often stops us being as successful as we might be? What so often stops us making our vision happen? What stops us being authentic – that is, true to our potential and the best version of that? Fear. And what so often is our biggest fear? The fear of failure.

Fear is an immensely powerful state. One which can immobilize and paralyze, which can cause us to have significant doubts. One which can cause chronic levels of anxiety. In many ways it seems to be a nuisance: we try and wish away fears before a presentation, or prior to a pay increase discussion or before we sign the document for our radical career move. But in fact we wouldn't want to do without it.

We wouldn't want to do without it? No, truly we wouldn't. Fear reminds us to proceed with caution, check what we can, plan where we are able. It isn't telling us *not* to do something, *not* to proceed. When you feel fear about the presentation you are about to give, if you are fearful about the rock climb you are about to undertake, it is natural. Literally. It's a wired-in mechanism. This state is actually saying: "Think. Are you ready? Have you planned? Are you poised?" And if you are not, it is encouraging you to do so. It is not, however, necessarily natural to proceed. You may decide the risks are in fact too great. To walk down that dark alleyway at two in the morning, although it reduces your walk home by twenty minutes, fills you with fear. Rightly so: don't do it. But with the presentation, or the climb, or that radical career move or the need to see your director about a bright idea you have, you can transform fear, you can get it to accompany you. Unfortunately that's where the real challenges lie. So often people stay immersed in the state of fear. Instead of using it to mobilize them, it freezes them. Fear tells us to proceed with caution to allow our comfort zone and our experience to expand. Fear is our guide. It ensures that we reduce the opportunity for grave errors to the minimum. It's thus a powerful and useful state. But once again, it's not there to stop us doing things, it's there to encourage us to do them in the correct way.

In our search for comfort we of course aim to remove discomfort. But as we remove discomfort we so often remove challenge. As we remove challenge we become bored – and we become uncomfortable. We encounter a paradox; clearly there are some comforts we would always want to have, like shelter or hot water. But what happens in our career if we insist on security? Will we turn down some options which might in the long term have given us more passion for the job? And with passion we can overcome the potential fear of insecurity.

In our current society many of us have become so comfortable that we have forgotten the importance of some stretch goals. That's what fear is: it's the extension, the stretch. So how do we overcome fear, we all want to know? We don't "overcome" it. We utilize it. We channel it. We work with it. How?

Stage 1

Realise that you are fearful. Feel that you are fearful. Slow down enough to register it fully. Don't try and hide it from yourself; don't rationalize, certainly don't camouflage it through busyness or drink. Notice what has happened to you, emotionally and physically. Immerse yourself in the fear. Don't talk yourself out of it. Just notice it. Stay with it. Now begin to decide that you wish to acknowledge the fear. What is it telling you? How can you use it? After all, you will be able to do so. Enjoy it. Enjoy noticing how fearful you are! Now go beyond the fear. You have noted what needs to be noticed so that you can now deliberately and consciously step beyond it.

Say you have been told that you need to present to the board. That is a significant step up from your previous level of presentation. Think about it – a lot – but be much more aware. Notice how and where you are feeling more fearful. Express your fears on paper. List them. As you do, you'll find they reduce to manageable proportions.

Susan Jeffers calls this the "feel the fear" stage.

Stage 2
Now, think for a moment: what is that fear doing? It's getting you to really focus. That's excellent. Now shift your mindset. Imagine that fear totally transformed into unstoppable energy. Let the fear really sit comfortably with you. Easier said than done, you might say. Ah – is that a limiting belief getting in the way?

Imagine that presentation; how would you be if you had tremendous energy? How would you be if you were focused? Now use that energy to get organized (see O for Organized). List exactly what you need to do. Prepare slides. Prepare notes. Build in several opportunities to rehearse. This will desensitize you to the fear.

Stage 3
Now decide. What are the pluses? What are the minuses? Should you just do it?

Decide if you are going ahead. Of course you are. What will you gain when you do? Get really clear on this – you'll get to meet the board and, more importantly, they'll get to see what you can do. They'll respect the fact that you're a bit nervous. You'll be on the way to being a serious presenter. What would you lose if you didn't do the presentation? You'd be fed up with yourself.

You'd reinforce a behaviour; you'd be running away from important areas of your life. You might never be asked to do it again.

Fear is about what might happen "if". And what might happen is that it works. If it doesn't, at least you have begun the process of anaesthetizing yourself to the "what if?" You have begun to widen your comfort zone.

And what about failure? Let's gather our thoughts:

We don't fail, we learn. If we strive to do our best and if things don't go to plan then that is simply an opportunity to learn.

If you see something as failure, think how you walk away. Think about your body language, your energy. That's right. It's not that great, is it? But now, what if you simply take the result as feedback and you're ready to learn and improve?

If fear of failure is our number one fear, what are our others? And how can we begin to manage them?

Fear of Public Speaking
1. The feeling of fear is saying "pay attention". Plan and prepare.

2. Plan and prepare again. Plan and prepare until it is wired-in. All professionals make it look easy and off the cuff through intensive preparation.

3. Start small; don't wait for the big one. Practice speaking to small groups, build up to larger and larger ones. Ask friends to ask questions and practice dealing with awkward customers.

4. Focus on your MEDS routine (see C for Compass). You'll speak and present a whole lot better if you have strength, stamina and relentless energy.

The fear of giving presentations – and of public speaking – is such a blocker on the route to excellence at senior corporate levels.

Geoff held a senior position and was very confident in many situations, but he had a particular fear and it was holding him back. It was the fear of keynote presentations: talking to his entire workforce of more than 750 people in one room at one time paralyzed him.

Consequently he avoided it. But unfortunately that meant he missed out on an excellent opportunity to rally the troops and talk to his staff.

Geoff's first challenge was that he simply would not accept the fear. He rationalized and did everything he could so that he neither discussed nor addressed it. As a consequence of this he was unwilling to give his problem any attention.

As he coached his young daughter in her first swimming lesson, Geoff realised that he was asking of her what he could not do himself. For his daughter to learn to swim and dive, she needed to accept that she was a little bit afraid and to manage that fear until she could overcome it.

Geoff did the same. He finally accepted, consciously and fully, that giving keynote speeches scared him stiff. And that was a huge relief for him.

Then, on that basis, he prepared carefully and thoroughly for his next speech. It was a success.

Fear of what others might think

1. It doesn't matter; see I for Internally-referenced. In essence you can never please everyone, neither at work nor in your social environment.

2. There will always be someone who wants to dumb down your life.

3. You'll be happiest when you are truly realising your potential and craft, not when you are doing things to keep someone else happy.

Fear of making a mistake, of getting it wrong

1. Accept that you will get things "wrong" but that doing so is simply learning. See *B for Beliefs*.

2. Practice getting it wrong and you'll get it right surprisingly often.

To support you in your mindset shifts, bear in mind the greater fears of not making the changes we anticipate. Don't be fearful of making the changes, or of speaking up or of making the decision. Be fearful of:

■ Looking back in old age and realising what you might have done and didn't...

■ Of finding it harder and harder to reveal "weaknesses" as one gets further into corporate life.

■ Failing to be a good "feel the fear and do it anyway" role model to your children.

■ Being someone who simply cannot cope with the hard times.

Stop making a fuss. Live alongside occasional discomfort.

Failure. You will fail. When you make changes it's unlikely that all will go to plan. And if it does go perfectly, maybe you have missed out on great learning. Remember that success is based on good judgment, that good judgment is based on experience and that experience is based on mistakes.

Feel the Fear and Do It Anyway. – SUSAN JEFFERS

G is Goal-Setting Formula

Goal-Setting

You know what? There is a formula for success! Yes, truly! Follow it and success will be yours! But just as with the genie and the lamp, there are simple words to be aware of...

1. Because it's a formula doesn't necessarily make it easy. The formula is well established, is not a secret patent and isn't magic. Despite that (perhaps because of that), you'll find that few people are using it.

2. You must be clear on what success is for you. "Loads of money" is not enough. I know you're getting the point on this. You must see clearly what you want. And start with the Compass Points.

3. You need to follow the formula stage by stage. Some people are just very poor at following directions. We're all for innovation, too. But follow the guidelines initially; it's much easier to innovate once you have got the basics.

4. You will need to put aside the limiting belief that if it were more complex the formula would somehow be more realistic. Simple does not mean simplistic. Complex does not mean realistic. Increasingly, in this complex world, we hide behind complexity. We see it in language: management-speak ("leverage the business model") corporate-speak, politics-speak, education-speak. In bureaucracy. In litigation. Go for simple. And the best "simple" is that which comes from wisdom: the simplicity, which exists on the far side of complexity.

Here goes.

Stage 1

Decide what success is for you. Know exactly what you want. I know you think that you have done a lot of work on this already; maybe, you feel, more than enough. Are you a little dubious? Do you feel that you have got this bit sorted already? May I test you?

I tell you what, try this exercise. Write non-stop for five minutes, describing exactly, in every way, what success will be like for you. Here are some examples.

Loads of money: Well, OK, how much? What will you be spending it on? Who will you share it with and what will be your first major expenditure? What would be your second? And where would you keep the money before you were able to spend it? Would you donate any to charity? Why? Why not?

Write a book: What is it called? Who is it for? What talk show would you like to be interviewed on? Which author would you like to have say "I loved this book?" What does the cover look like? In which countries would it be sold?

Lose weight: From where? All over? Stomach? Bottom? How much? By when? For what reason? How are you going to do it? Starve ? Really? Run? Oh, really? What will be your running route? What do you expect your run time to be? What time will you start your run? And will it be every day?

Off you go. Now. A timed five minutes of continuous writing. If you stop, deduct that time until you have done the full five minutes.

Interesting, isn't it? Congratulations if your flow of writing was fast, lucid and particularly explicit. You have a crystal clear picture of what you want. And that, as we have begun to see and shall continue to see, is a very large part of the battle. We need to create mentally, first, before we can create physically, second. If you have a clear mental image then you can probably make it happen physically. But maybe you struggled significantly. Maybe you couldn't answer the questions. Maybe you found it boring. Well, what does that tell you? That Stage 1 is not ready yet. You need to focus further, give it more attention, get that first stage correct. Stand up. Do that now. Stretch. Go for a walk. Come back and write again. And again. If it helps, include pictures. But don't stop until you have that absolute, explicit clarity which belongs to someone who has passion for what they want to achieve.

So, for Stage 1, firstly get a "sensory rich" image. Secondly, check it's what you want, not what you don't want. I know that might seem silly, but for many hopes of success are what they *don't* want. "I don't want to be so fat." (OK, so what do you want? To be slim – whatever that means – or to lose a specific amount?) "I don't want to have to work here." (OK, where would you like to work?) "I don't want to stay so late." (OK, so what time would you like to leave?) You need a positive affirmation of what you do want because:

■ A positive is measurable. I can measure "I want to get home at 6 p.m." It's more difficult to measure "I don't want to stay so late at work."

■ We give the brain a negative command, which doesn't work. Have you ever tried *not* to think about gorillas after someone asked you to do just that? Not being fat is tricky. Losing 10 lbs is achievable.

If you draw, your clear sensory image will default to what you want. After all, it's tricky to draw a picture of not being fat.

To recap on Stage 1: Decide clearly, explicitly, in a sensory rich way, what you do want (and of course, *not* what you don't want).

Stage 2

Now try – have a go. Start the process. Losing weight. Painting. To do this, you'll use a strategy. Now for many of us our strategy is unconscious; we just have a go. Or sometimes we do deliberately try and do it in a certain way. Thus, to get a new job we look through the employment ads and respond to appropriate ones. Not a bad strategy. When we wish to lose weight we simply don't eat anything containing sugar. Not a bad strategy. If our strategy works then clearly it has a lot to be said for it. But it may not work or we may be keen to get a more effective strategy.

But where do we get the strategy from? An excellent source is from someone who is good at the process. Find them, then replicate their strategy. For instance if you want to be good at running meetings, note what someone who is excellent at the process does. Maybe you will find a colleague who has been very successful at getting great jobs by being proactive, by not just responding to ads but actually writing to companies they would like to work for. Ask yourself this question: what do people who have achieved the result that you are also seeking actually do (as opposed to what they say they do, or think they do)?

For example, say one of your goals is to become great at managing meetings. What you want is to "become excellent at running business meetings". Presumably you will have some kind of personal benchmark on this so that you will know which areas you want to improve. So, find someone who is good and ask them how they do it.

Tips:
1. Work hard to get people to describe what they actually do, rather than what they think they do. This is a great reason for observing them "at work".
2. Of course, some people will be too busy. So remember "no" is not "no, not ever". It is "no, not now". Be persistent. Politely ask when you could get ten minutes of their time.
3. Thank them and drop them a note mentioning some of the benefits of their help.

Stage 3
This stage is where you begin to notice feedback. Are you happy with what is happening? Is your saving scheme working? Are you getting fitter? Are you feeling more comfortable with this new way of managing the team?

If it's going well, continue. Be persistent. You will probably notice an even greater return. But if it's not working, then don't forget to change the strategy because maybe this strategy is not a good one, or not a good one for you, or not a good one now. So change it, edit it. Talk to your learning team. Do some networking (see L for Lifelong Learning).

Stage 4 – Hey! Success!
Will you need discipline to keep this going? No, not necessarily. What is important is routine. Whatever it is that you are seeking, make it a routine. A new career? Keep reading, networking, doing proactive applications, applying the A to Z. And couple that with simplicity of strategy.

And that's it.

You know the number of people who say that they want to write a book and then you find that they have never put pen to paper?

Penny had always wanted to write a book. She knew it was in her, but she couldn't get it out. She had set a goal: to write a book by Easter 2003. She'd been careful not to overstate her case, as in "write a bestseller," but she still hadn't written the book. In fact she hadn't done any writing at all. Then her sister gave her a copy of *The Artist's Way* by Julia Cameron and Penny realised the flaw in her plan: she didn't actually know how to start writing. She didn't have any kind of strategy.

Julia Cameron gave her one: "Write!" No fuss, no excuses. Just write. So Penny did. Every morning she wrote and wrote. Eventually she edited and edited. And one day she had a manuscript. She wrote to thirty agents. Two were interested. She selected one. Her agent wrote to five publishers without success. Penny rewrote the ending of her story and submitted it to five more publishers. Finally it was accepted for publication.

She was a writer at last. But only once she had clicked to the Goal-Setting Formula.

"Just as with the genie and the lamp, there are simple words to be aware of..."

H is Hero

Hero

We all admire a hero. What is a hero? Somebody who does that extra something. Somebody who does what is necessary, something which captures our mind and stirs our heart. And they do it when perhaps the odds are against them and others are fearful. They come in all walks of life, with a range of qualities. One quality is to have the courage to do what is necessary, when it is necessary.

What if you were a hero? No, no need for the dramatic felling of a bank robber or the reviving of a cardiac-arrest victim. No, closer to home. What if, despite everything apparently being against you – "no time to write," or "I'm overweight" or "business sales are falling month by month" – you turned it around? Or in your committee meeting, what if you spoke out on that contentious issue? You did what was necessary? How about if you were a silent hero as well? You made no fuss. You expected no congratulations. You managed your ego. You just did it because it is important. Yep, you're right. It would be cool.

Do you have the hero's courage, the hero's clarity to make some changes? Can you overcome your addiction to smoking, for example? Or stand up to the office bullying which is occurring? Or simply get up half an hour earlier to write? The good news is that you know that you can; that is, you physically can. The question is will you choose to do so? Will you take on – in your own particular way – the mindset of a hero?

Here's a more personal story.

Last year on a bitterly cold December morning I stopped to buy a magazine from the local *Big Issue* seller. He looked very cold; I asked him how it was going. He was cheerful – as ever – but told me that when he had arrived "on patch" that morning outside M&S someone was sleeping where he normally stood. And that person, covered in frost, had clearly been there all night.

The *Big Issue* seller got the sleeper up and took him for breakfast at a café; he didn't have enough for one himself, and to earn that money he would have to sell an extra seven magazines.

That's a hero. Doing what's important, even when it's uncomfortable, difficult or close to impossible.

Decide to become a hero. A hero is represented strongly by the first seven characteristics of the A to Z. This would be a good time to review them and look at them afresh, from the perspective of a hero.

Attention

A hero focuses consistently on the issues which need to be addressed. There is no defensiveness, no rationalization, no blame. Just simple attention. If, after long consideration, the business can only be turned around through some radical reinvention, then so be it. If that chronic fatigue from which you are currently suffering is only going to be solved by a significant change in lifestyle, perhaps leaving your current prestigious job, then so be it. Or more simply, even if buying a copy of the *Big Issue* each week will help erode your cynicism to those less well off – then do it. Yes,

I know you need to stop and find some change and you're in a hurry and... Just do it. See K.

Attention is all for a hero. Make it happen.

Beliefs
A hero holds a particular set of beliefs. He or she certainly uses all seven beliefs which we have already studied in B for Belief. Two additional hero beliefs are:

- "I can make a difference." So often we simply rationalize our inactivity suggesting it won't make any difference at all. It will. Small efforts create ripples. Others notice. In particular, you notice and do more. Just do it and make a difference.

- "I am bigger than this issue." Sometimes we need to recognize we are simply being too melodramatic. We can step beyond a particular issue. Maybe, of course, with help – but we can do it.

Above all, heroes regularly remind themselves that their beliefs dictate their behaviours which dictate their results.

Compass clarity
A hero has clarity. A hero has direction. A hero knows what he or she needs to do. And they realise that this arises from their LifeCompass^{SM}.

In particular:

■ **Compass Point 1:** career. Heroes think beyond a job (something done just to earn cash), beyond a career (something done for the money, security and pension), beyond a vocation (something done because "it fits") to a passion: something which gets you out of bed in the morning, something which supports your contributory activity, something which supports your skill, and something which pays you well and – above all – something which gives you a passion for life.

Heroes live with a passion, for a passion.

■ **Compass Point 2:** mind/body. A hero recognizes that they will be able to achieve very little unless their mind/body is in a peak state; they train their body, they train their mind. In their own particular way, whether that be by running, walking, cycling, swimming, reading or discussion. No big deal; they find their particular way for energy.

■ **Compass Point 3:** finance. A hero is not distracted by the side issue of poorly-managed finances. They get this "personal finance" out of the way. They are able to manage their personal debt, clear it and take the necessary action to build personal wealth for the future. Above all a hero realises that this compass point is truly about affluence and that affluence often only requires a small contribution from money.

■ **Compass Point 4:** relationships. Heroes respect those around them. They are careful to balance their own passions and things they must do with those who don't hold those passions or who even fundamentally disagree with them. They respect the differing opinions of others. They encourage their life partner to live their life fully. They encourage their children to develop their independence in an atmosphere of unconditional love.

■ **Compass Point 5:** fun. Heroes have a light-heartedness. They can have child-like fun. They have a love of romance: a carefully prepared meal for a loved one. Of adventure: using a new language in a new country. The adventure of "ordinary stuff" such as taking a child camping.

■ **Compass Point 6:** contribution. Heroes think beyond themselves: from small things such as recycling bottles to supporting a charity, to speaking out against a corrupt government.

Decision

Heroes are decision makers. And importantly they are practical decision makers; they do stuff. They realise that it is easy to remain intellectual. They realise that the decision they make might not be the right decision – but they do realise that they are, in fact, making progress.

They practice making decisions so that this is something they live and breathe. They recognize that simply because a decision is tough is not a reason for putting it off.

EQ: emotional intelligence

Heroes are not robots. They realise that so much of what they need to do is not based around a project plan or a checklist of a set of metrics; it is dependent upon relationships. The busyness of many of our personal lives and the competitive pressures of our business lives often removes the simplest of emotions from everyday interactions. You know that a simple "thank you" at the right time can be the most motivating thing you can say.

Fear

Heroes are fearless. No, not true! Heroes use their fear. They use that organic and intrinsic fear which they will never let go; they use it to help them focus, find passion and "get-up-in-the-morning unstoppability".

GSF: Goal-Setting Formula

A hero follows the formula: aim, fire, feedback. Aim, fire and more feedback. Aim, fire, bull's-eye!

Above all, "hero" is a state of mind. It is something which you can choose to do, something which will allow you to step above/step over any trivial problems you may come across.

Decide to be a hero. Use the strategy of "act as if". When you realise that a hero's mindset would be an ideal one for a situation, ask yourself, "What would a true hero do now? How would they behave?" And do what is necessary.

"Have the courage to do what is necessary, when it is necessary."

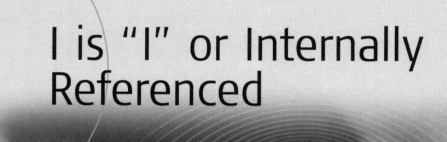

I is "I" or Internally Referenced

It may have struck you, while considering these characteristics, "When I make these changes, what might people think? That I am stupid? Gullible? To be admired? Will they be supportive?" Or "How much should I consider the opinions of others when I make changes?" These are not easy points to consider. People will not always be supportive. Some will, but some may try very hard to talk you out of your plans; more on this in a moment. And in some situations, it is vital to consider the opinions of others, especially those closest to you.

When we make changes, people around us do notice. Sometimes they are amazingly supportive and encouraging. Other times they can be dismissive and off-hand. Why the latter behaviour? One possibility is certainly that they genuinely feel that you have been hoodwinked, talked into some change which is not really you. Who are you, after all, to suddenly feel you could become manger of the local Internet Cafe? And then they want to "rescue" you. However, often the reasons are more concerning: because they feel threatened. Threatened, yes, in several possible ways. Firstly if you achieve this change, maybe it indicates that they could make some of the changes they claim that they would like but about which have been making excuses; this can cause them deep discomfort. An easy way to get rid of the discomfort is to dissuade you from making the change at all. Secondly, if you do change then they may feel that they will lose you, perhaps literally or perhaps on a mental level. Again, to avoid this loss, a good start is to dissuade you from making the changes in the first place.

The key for you is to become internally rather than externally referenced. Realise that nobody is losing you, in particular *you* are not losing you! Others will be gaining the true you, the authentic you. But more importantly, you will be gaining the true you. When you are internally-referenced you stay true to your inner core and what is truly important. Of course, don't be selfish, nor should you ignore feedback. However, when you are externally referenced you will be swayed by any comment; you will never discover the true you.

Let's give a simple example. It's been a hectic weekend and you are partied out; time for a couple of days detox, you decide. On Tuesday night a friend invites you to the pub to meet up with some of your other friends. You say you'll go, but add that you do not want to drink anything alcoholic. The question is how you react when you get to the pub and are bullied by your friends to have an alcoholic drink. If you stay principled and say no, you're internally-referenced. If you say yes, you're externally referenced.

When you become internally-referenced you stop trying to be someone else. By all means learn from others. But stop trying to be someone else. Be yourself and simply become better at that. As you do this a true passion for work and life develops. Daily work appears in a more "flow" state, less fragmented and not such hard work. That's because Be is so much more important that Do. To have, you must Do. But to Do, you must Be. And most importantly you must be yourself. But – and there is a big *but* here – this may be OK for casual friends, for distant relatives, but what about those who are closest to you? Those who worry about damaging, or even worse precipitating the end of, a great relationship? This is not easy at all. But do remember that relationships are organic and will shift and change over time: that's healthy and normal. And it's likely that your respective personal development paths will be moving at different rates. Stay loving, stay supportive and in general there is no reason why your relationship needn't become stronger than it has ever been. As you become more true to yourself, you can become more true to others.

Pressure from society and political correctness all put more pressures on those who want to do things in a particular way. One area sure to cause debate is, of course, bringing up children. I'm amazed at the strong reactions I get if I mention that we don't have a TV in the house. Mind you, that's nothing compared to this.

Sue had had enough. It had been hard enough to stick to her decision to leave work when she became pregnant, and then to stick to her determination to stay at home with the baby. "But you'll be so bored. You'll miss the buzz of this place!" her colleagues told her. Most insistent were those who, having returned to work after the minimum maternity leave placing the baby in the workplace nursery, now juggled children, home and career with apparent success. "I couldn't bear to spend all day with toddlers," some cried, "I'd go out of my mind."
Sue had to admit that this had got to her. What if bringing up her own children was not as fascinating and worthwhile as she dreamed? What if other people ignored her, thought she had become stupid and boring without a career? Maybe she would lose her friends, her figure and her mind.

But she persisted and a few supporters had come out of the woodwork. They shared their experience of being brow-beaten into taking a path that was not right for them and encouraged her to do what she felt was the right thing.

Then her son was born. She had never anticipated the problems associated with breastfeeding, nor the well-meaning comments that would undermine her best efforts. From her mother: "He seems hungry. Are you sure you've got enough milk? Why not give him a little extra bottle?" Her friends: "It really limits you! And you're beginning to smell of milk! What have you got against bottles anyway, it's the twenty-first century, you're not telling me they can't make a perfectly good formula milk." Her health visitor: "Well, dear, breastfeeding doesn't work for everyone, and you've given him all the benefits by feeding for the first week." Her husband: "You look so tired. Surely if you tried a bottle I could take over and you could sleep in." The Sunday papers: "Only eight percent of British mothers persist in breastfeeding for more than six weeks."

She was sick of it. She believed in breastfeeding. She wanted to do it. And she would, never mind what others thought.

And she did. She contacted an NCT breastfeeding counsellor to get the advice she needed and she breastfed her son successfully for almost a year. That's being internally-referenced.

Here are some specific tactics to help your move to becoming more internally referenced.

Tactic 1: know what you want

You'll be noticing how much we keep coming back to this point. The emphasis here is particularly on what *you* want; be careful of responding to what others want for you. If you want to be an actor, go for it. Yes, everyone will tell you that...

Focus here on C for Compass. When you know what you want you can say "yes" to that which supports you and "no" to that which doesn't. When you haven't set your Personal Compass, it can be very difficult to avoid being taken along by the crowd.

It has been said that you can always say no when you have a bigger yes inside.

Tactic 2: develop personal strength and passion

Work on Compass Point 2: mind/body, particularly MEDS. You need strength and stamina to get the changes that you want to happen and to combat the negativity of others. Do this both mentally and physically. Mentally, be careful about labelling yourself and being worried by your labels. A label? A label is a job title or a description you have become known by; perhaps people think of you as "the quiet one" or you're a "small d" director. What does that label do to you? Does it weaken you or make you more powerful? Just because of some (often) ill-chosen words!

Notice how much energy some give to concern over personal labels or job titles or just having the right qualifications. An MBA is a big time-and-money investment. Could you get better benefits in one-hundredth of the time by reading the right books, networking, developing a great attitude and understanding self-invention and personal marketing? Perhaps.

Tactic 3: develop your assertiveness

Being assertive means protecting your rights. You're right to have a different opinion, for example. Aggressive people transgress your rights. Don't allow them to do so. Passive people do not respect their own rights: don't allow that to happen to you. So how do you go about developing your assertiveness?

Assertiveness revolves around respecting rights – on both sides of the conversation. Some rights are fundamental; for instance, the right to explore a view, go home on time without feeling guilty, be treated with courtesy. Some are job-dependent: what authority level do I have? And of course it is a basic right to understand one's job rights.

Our goal, when being assertive, is to respect rights on both sides of the conversation. Someone who is aggressive is respecting their own rights but not those of others. Someone who is passive is not respecting their own rights. Both are short-term strategies likely to lead to long-term difficulties.

Tactic 4: focus on your self-development
As you grow, all of these ideas become easier. Resist the temptation to judge others on their development path. They may not be ready to make the changes you wish to make, yet. Or they may be on a different path which will link with yours in a different way.

Tactic 5: think particularly about Y for Yin and Yang, and Z for Zen and the Art of Being Successful...

"When I make
these changes,
what might
people think?"

J

J is Journey

Journey

Because you are reading this book you are probably an "achiever" already. Achievers are usually interested in how they can achieve more. Their desire to do this is measured in their constant quest to "get there", for "perfection", for "certainty".

However, your happiness, your growth, will depend as much if not more upon the journey you make to your goal rather than on the destination, the goal itself. You may have noticed how sometimes the planning of the theatre trip, the birthday surprise, the new product configuration can be as much fun as the actual event (sometimes even more fun); how once you have achieved your goal things can – at times – seem a little flat; until, of course, you discover your next goal. For many of us, realising this can be a significant change in thinking. The good news is that it can make our life a whole lot easier. In general there's a whole lot more journey around than there is destination! Let's look at how it might work.

When running a small business we may think our goal is to close deals (the destination). Although we undoubtedly need to keep that in mind, more importantly we actually want to become a natural choice in our sector of the market (our journey). Then business will become a lot easier. If we simply chase closed deals we may well miss the point of our service and product to customers. In fact we may do well in the short term but actually create our own demise in the longer term.

When getting married we can easily (because of the natural fun and excitement) begin to think that it is all about the wedding day (the apparent destination). In fact it's all about the journey of our life together. Sometimes the stress of that "perfect" day does irreparable damage to the start of the relationship.

In our business and personal lives, the journey is more significant and more critical than our destination. If we focus on the journey and take the correct one, then the destination will work out. How many times have you noticed that the plot has been totally lost; the customer service metrics have become more important than the actual customer service?

When we set our heart on something, we should ask what it is really about.

So, take "I want to write a book" (destination). Is that about a journey of self-expression, changing the world, making more money? Or about what? Because once we know we can a) get it more clearly, and b) find other routes. Are you writing a book or a journal? Do you want to learn a language? Or stretch your brain or meet new people?

Or "I want to make a million by the time I'm 30." Is that about a journey of money, self-expression? Self-worth, contribution?

As you do this, you begin to discover the true journeys that you want to make. Maybe for you the journey is one of self-expression, or of achievement or of contribution. And by noticing those themes you find you can get more precise about your destination.

Journey thinking

■ Enjoy what you are doing now, rather than constantly seeking the next stage: enjoy the holiday now, worry about work later. Be in the moment rather than be concerned about the next one.

■ Learn as you go, rather than simply learning on the result: build your curiosity and constantly improve through constant learning.

■ Measure yourself on your growth and investment rather than simply on your achievements: think of yourself as an organization. How's your balance sheet? Is it strengthening or weakening?

■ Do less to achieve more: stop rushing around. Slow down and think: "What's important here?" For example, "Why are we running this exhibition? Is it the appearance of the stand which is most crucial, or is it more about actually making contact with our customers?"

■ Focus on compass: realise that the important, truly important, aspects of your life are investing, journey tasks.

Destination Thinking

Destination thinkers:

■ Enjoy only small parts of projects

■ Put emphasis on urgency and adrenaline. They will often say that they need a "buzz" to get them to achieve. How about the buzz of quality or full understanding?

■ Do more and achieve less.

■ Emphasize goals and the measurable. One of the biggest disasters of modern thinking is to assume that if we are to make headway, something must be strictly measurable. Not necessarily. Attempting to measure often distracts us from what is truly important. Even worse, in the search for what is measurable we take the easily measurable; the number of sales calls, for instance, rather than the quality of those sales calls.

■ Focus on the clock

It's so easy to lose the plot. Here's a story from one couple.

Morgan and Siobhan wanted the best for their children as they grew up; the things they themselves had not had. Their own bedrooms. Their own TV and CD players. Decent holidays where the sun shone. Private schools. To do all that, of course, they would both need to work, but they would be able to ensure their children had a place in the best nursery; they could check the children on the cam link and the nutrition charts showed that they were better fed, almost, than if they had been at home.

It was hard in the evenings. They were both very tired and although the supermarket's organic, microwaveable foods were excellent – every evening?!

And the weekends were hell. They knew they ought to be spending more quality time with the children, but to be honest they seemed happier watching the video and TV which allowed Siobhan and Morgan to have a much-needed lie in. Every interaction with the children seemed to be a struggle, and yet the last thing they wanted to do was to spend their precious weekends laying down the law; it seemed easier to let things go, and yet each of them had a sneaking feeling that the children were becoming demanding little strangers.

Then one day Siobhan heard a comment in the supermarket and it changed her life. A man and woman were in the process of a discussion. The man was saying, "Well, if it's so tough financially, why don't we try to entertain the kids this weekend without spending any money? How about if we use what's in the house? On Saturday morning we could make bread – all of us. Make it fun. And lunch could be beans on toast."

Siobhan's evening was not easy, but eventually she convinced Morgan that a change was necessary, otherwise a day would come when their children would be teenagers who regarded their parents as no more than well-meaning bank managers.

They did it. It took them nine months. They slashed their budget. They created two part-time jobs. They spent more time with each other and with the children.

They were enjoying the journey again; the destination would work out.

Be a journey traveller rather than a destination wisher.

K is Killer App

There is one ultimate, definitive way of getting the success you want. One ultimate, definitive "killer app". And that is JFDI. JUST F*C*ING DO IT!

My apologies if that seems overly direct, despite the asterisks. But there is a tendency for some individuals to become so fascinated with how they might change, and with their preparation and planning, that they never get around to actually *doing* anything!

There comes a point when there are no more techniques, no more books to read, no more courses to attend, no need for more planning. There is, however, a desperate need simply to tackle the issues. Simply do it. If for no other reason than to begin to wire your body into making changes: no procrastination; just do it. Get your mind/body used to making changes: radically adjust that currently lethargic, action-taking "muscle memory".

So what are your challenges? What is stopping you from simply doing it? Experience (from my coaching sessions and workshops) suggests it is probably one of the following top ten challenges or blockers which people commonly appear to face. They tend to be expressed like this:

1. **No time** – "I simply can't find the dedicated time to address it."

2. **No energy** – "I just slump in the evenings."

3. **Not now** – "It'll be easier next year."

4. **What will people think?** – "They might think I'm a bit of a corporate creep."

5. **What happens if it doesn't work?** – "I might look silly."

6. **Lack of resources** – "I don't have enough resources, particularly money."

7. **Procrastination** – "I'm stuck and I don't know which way to go."

8. **Fear** – "I'd love to, but..."

9. **Labelling** – "I think I'm the kind of person who needs to..."
   (Insert label here, like "think about it for a while.")

10. Any other excuse you can think of!

These are all ideal for the JFDI approach, which goes like this:

JUST
No more discussion, get up, go to the person, go to the phone, whatever is necessary. Move from thought to action. This may seem too simplistic to you, but it absolutely works; as you move you develop more energy for more action. Change your physiology and consequently change your thinking. Have you ever been powerfully action-orientated while slumped in a chair? No, thought not. Have you ever felt really good while walking along, head down, hands in pockets? No! Realise your physiology will support, or undermine, your effectiveness.

F*C*ING

Put some energy into it. Assume a state of "nothing is going to stop me". This is the state of "Don't mess with me. I'm going to make this happen!" How would you be – your physiology, your tonality – if you were unstoppable?

DO

Do equals action. That's what's needed now. You have to do before you can have. Take an action.

IT!

And do you know what "it" is? I'm really trusting that you have got very specific on this! If you haven't, then go back to C for Compass.
Now let's resolve each of those potential blockers we listed above.

1. No time

As in "I simply can't find the dedicated time to address it." You never will have sufficient dedicated time. Creative, intelligent people have never got enough time. It's a given, so accept it and stop complaining. Maybe that surprises you? Maybe you thought I was going to give you an explanation of how to have plenty of time! No – I'll be showing you how to get the results you want. And that's a very different requirement. Break the connection between time and results. Realise that you don't necessarily need lots of time for lots of results. You need focused time for excellent results. Here's what you do. You honestly admit to yourself that your diary is certainly not optimized at the moment. Recognize that you could do any of the following, amongst other ideas:

■ Get up half an hour earlier three times a week.

■ Watch 50 percent less television.

■ Cut down on some of the "social grease" at work.

■ Write a shopping list to reduce wasted time during your trip to the supermarket.

And with that new-found time, start doing the stuff you both want and need to do. Watch out for that word "dedicated". Big chunks of time are a luxury. Sure, have your "Awaydays", book your retreats to do your writing. But also get pragmatic about just doing stuff in smaller chunks of time.

No, you may never have enough time. But you can always get direction. You have the ability to choose. Do so.

2. No energy

Refer back to your compass, particularly Compass Point 2: mind/body. Re-read MEDS. Check that you are tackling all four aspects for real energy. Also notice the expression "I just slump once I have done the essentials." How about making this particular change you require one of the essentials? We all have time for what is truly necessary; make one of the essentials getting your energy back!

Remember that complaining is debilitating. Action is enthusing and progressing. Passion and enthusiasm are self-fulfilling and generate more passion and energy.

3. Not now

"It'll get easier next year." You know that you are kidding yourself, now is the perfect time. If you leave it you know it'll only get harder. Watch out for "Soon it'll get easier!" It won't, you know! How many facts do you want? A recent DTI report suggested that world knowledge is currently doubling every five years but that by the year 2020 it will be doing so every 73 days. In the nineteenth century an educated man or woman would have had as much new knowledge to contend with in the whole of their lifetime as we might have in one day. You know it won't get any easier. Today is the day to start making the change that you seek.

4. What will people think?

"They might think I'm a bit of a corporate creep." They might. But that says a lot more about them than about you. Anyway, they may be impressed. They may be resentful. It really doesn't matter. Do it anyway.

Don't try and be liked by everyone in your life. In work, try and win respect; that means that you will be regularly taking tough decisions. Above all, don't dumb down your life.

5. What happens if it doesn't work?

"I might look silly." It probably won't go to the full, 100 percent success as you would have hoped. Never mind anyway. From B for Beliefs you know that that is only feedback. And don't worry about looking silly. You won't look half as silly as the ones who don't have a job in 18 months' time, nor as silly as the ones who have never ever taken a risk and are becoming less and less attractive recruitment prospects.

6. Lack of resources

"I don't have enough resources, particularly money." When have you ever had enough money? Quite. What can you do without money? Can you create the plan? And if you definitely do need money then that becomes your number one goal. Making money.

Distinguish carefully between having resources and being resourceful. You don't have the resources, but you can certainly always be resourceful. By resourceful, we mean having the ability to work out what we might do. Stop whinging and be proactive. What can you influence?

7. Procrastination

"I'm stuck and I don't know which way to go." Brainstorm all the options thoroughly and then follow your gut feeling. Take action, any action. Go for a walk.

One thing is for sure. If you stay in that state, then you will certainly stay stuck. And if you get into that unresourceful state very often you will find that it is a seductively easy one to slip into. Dangerous! Break the pattern; go for a walk, talk to or email someone. Get a large sheet of paper, write ideas, promise yourself that you will get going again.

8. Fear

"I'd love to, but..." Try "I'd love to, and I *will* have a go" instead. Here's the message: get off your "but". Replace it with "and". And have a go.

9. Labelling

"I think I'm the kind of person who needs to..." (Insert label here, like "think about it for a while.") Ignore the label. It'll be incorrect, a generalization from a one-off experience. Labels come from all over the place. Some are from work ("trainee" sales consultant). Some are from parents or school ("you're lazy"). Some are self-generated ("I'm simply not the kind of person to speak out in a meeting").

Steam that label off. Get a better label such as: "I'm progressing," or "I'm working on it" or "My badge may say trainee, but I'm a future MD."

10. Any other excuse you can think of!

I think you get the message. You can always find an excuse. And the answer is not to accept the excuse; recognize it as for what it is: a blocker to you realising and releasing your full potential. And comments about the "real world" and "it's OK for them" – drop them. Re-focus on the Goal-Setting Formula. And apply the Killer App with a vengeance.

JFDI
ANON

L is Lifelong Learning

Learning

L is for Lifelong Learning. Recognize that an important quality of compass time is personal investment. Your future employability is a direct correlation of your current learning. There was a time – and for some of us this is within living memory – when there was very little change year on year. Once a bank manager, always a bank manager. One year a trainee sales consultant, two years later a senior account manager. CVs built neatly and steadily in length and weight. Now it's all change. We're only as good as our last gig.

Learning never stops. For many of us there are aspects of our job for which our knowledge half-life (the time in which half of our knowledge is outdated) is very short. For example, once in marketing it was good enough to sell a service, now increasingly the customer wants an experience; have you been keeping up-to-date with current thinking on how to respond to that? In customer service it was enough to offer a money-back guarantee. Now everyone does that, so what will you do to distinguish yourself? Break the connection between learning and college or learning and "courses". Realise that whatever your job, whatever your career, the relentless rate of change is stripping the automation from your job as quickly as it can. You must build the true "knowledge, intelligence and attitude" aspects of your job that cannot be converted into a computer-driven menu system, so that you are always needed. And certainly break the link between your learning and it being someone else's responsibility.

Here are some strategies for becoming a Lifelong Learner.

1. **Remember that life is a free, top quality development program.** Everything that happens to you is a potential learning experience: not getting the promotion you wanted, breaking your leg on your first skiing trip. Remember to enroll fully in the course, do your

homework, study the "marking". Be accepting and don't be defensive. If you do that, you'll learn hugely each and every day. Here's a fun yet powerful belief to use when things don't seem to go your way: OK – what is the universe trying to tell me here? And notice that sometimes the universe will keep telling you until you get the message!

When you complete a project insist on a detailed review of what went well and what went less well. If you are ever given a poor review or told off, ask for specifics that would help you to avoid the mistake in the future.

Get a notebook. Make it an attractive one. Spiral? A4? A5? What would work best for you? Carry this notebook and a pencil with you at all times. Get used to jotting down thoughts and observations. Be reflective. Read these points back to yourself. Notice how much you develop and improve. Write down references to books, quotations, websites. Follow up, follow through.

2. Read widely. There has never been a better time to find a wide selection of excellent books in the area of personal development. Make a decision always to be reading one; attempt to read such a book for fifteen minutes every day. If you use any kind of public transport then that is certainly possible. However, don't beat yourself up. So many people say "I've got a stack of books by my bedside table, but I've not touched any of them" – they are trying to read all of each book. Don't do that. Just try and read some of them and/or some chapters of some of them. Find a favourite bookstore to which you can retreat sometimes, where you can chill out and dip into books. Get organized with your favourite online book store. Set yourself a book budget; always spend it and as your career develops, increase the proportion of your salary you spend on books. Stuck for money for books? Consider ditching your daily newspaper. Twenty daily newspapers will buy you a good personal development book. Or how about one night less in the pub per week?

Listen to audio books. If you do a lot of driving you can certainly use the time then. With these in particular, consider setting up a library in your mini-team.

Here are six classics to read:

- Stephen R Covey, *The 7 Habits of Highly Effective People*. A classic in the personal development field. Great structure, great stories. Easy to implement.
- M. Scott Peck. *The Road Less Travelled*. Excellent piece of work on the role of personal responsibility.
- Try *Frogs into Princes* by Richard Bandler and John Grinder. NLP, but from the originals.
- Ken and Kate Back, *Assertiveness at Work*. Immensely practical on a life-changing, if non-sexy, skill.
- Richard Nelson Bolles, *What Color is your Parachute?* The original job hunters' or career mangers' guide.
- Deepak Chopra, *Perfect Health*. The definitive mind/body book.

Once you have tried these, read something out of your mainstream. For instance try *Complications*, by Atul Gawande; read biographies – political, sporting, historical – or find something from the reading lists in any of the classics mentioned above.

And here's a mildly contentious point: would you "mark up" your own book? That's up to you, I believe. Once marked it will be a distraction in the future. But if it's just for you, for reference, then what the heck?

Take notes; use your notebook. Note interesting points, great quotations. Other books which you would like to follow up. Make your notebook attractive to you – scan it every so often. If you are thinking of becoming a writer, this will be particularly important to you.

As you take notes, think about the skills you have on the critical path of learning, reading and note-taking. Here are some tips.

Reading

If you want just the essence of a book, then try the Pareto approach: just read the first and last sentence of every paragraph. From that 20 percent you will get 80 percent of the meaning. For further understanding, read as usual but be proactive. Try and increase your reading speed, for instance, without losing understanding.

Note-taking.

If you are happy to mark your book, then use a fluorescent highlighter. But use it sparingly. Summarize each chapter following reading, but do this in the inside front cover.

3. **Attend every development program your organization offers; keep the brain active.** Equally, though, don't wait if your company doesn't send you on anything; book on a great course yourself. If a course is running during the business week and your company won't send you, consider taking a few days vacation to attend.

Get maximum value from the course: read beforehand, ask questions during it and follow-up afterwards.

Set yourself a personal budget for your training courses. Ask for funding from work or at least for a contribution.

4. Set up a Learning Team. This is a team dedicated to learning which meets every month for one hour to act as a catalyst to learning. Here are the rules:

- No social grease; it's purely for learning.
- Everyone brings along some material to do some teaching.

The majority of my clients love their Learning Teams once they have established them.

Annette was part of a Lifelong Learning Team. It was just one hour per month, but she loved it. She was really trying to cope with her depression since the break-up of a long-term relationship and the team meetings really helped. No sympathy, no social chat, just practical work.

This month's topic was health. They had mutually decided that it would be a good topic, and although Annette hadn't discussed her depression they had all decided that they would love to be a lot healthier. Annette was excited when one of the group shared some readings from a book called *Potatoes, not Prozac.* Maybe here was a way she could tackle her problem without the drug she was currently taking.

Three months later Annette was no longer taking Prozac. A changed diet – and being a lifelong learner – had done the trick.

5. Network. Keep tabs on all your contacts. Speak to them every so often. Pass on information which is relevant to them. You'll notice that they do the same for you.

6. Create a study area. Anywhere. A good desk space. A great lamp. Perhaps a plant or two. Shelves for books. A CD/tape player.

7. Key Skills. As a lifelong learner, here are the skills which will be vital to you where ever you take your career.

■ *Leadership* (meeting management/parenting/running your own company).
   - Know how to lead yourself.
   - Know how to lead others.

■ *Customer Service (partnering).*
   - Understand the balance of IQ/EQ in the customer engagement situation.
   - Specifics such as rapport.

■ *Selling.*
   - How to present benefits in financial, functional, short term and long term.
   - How to influence a Decision Making Unit.

■ *Presenting.*
   - Able to do so one to one, and one to many.

■ *Assertiveness.*

- *Finance.*
  - P&L.
  - Cash flow.
  - What is profit?

- *Study Skills.*
  - Accelerated reading.
  - Accelerated note-taking.

8. Action Planning. Get used to carrying a 3x5 card with you on which you have written two to three areas of development to which you wish to give attention, for example
  - learn people's names in meetings this week
  - push back at cost-reduction sessions
  - take 45 minutes break every lunchtime.

Focus on this every day; these are the areas you are currently working on. Perhaps you are developing your assertiveness, perhaps preparing for a Learning Team session.

Review it at the end of the day. Tick those achieved. Forget the others or roll them over to another day. File the cards. Once a month take them all out and notice the progress that you have made.

Forget to remember the stuff you don't need any more.
RICHARD BANDLER

M is Motivation

Motivation is not something that just happens to you. Nor is it something that "sometimes you have, and sometimes you haven't". Should you rely on some kind of carrot to create it? If someone offers us a lot of money to do the ironing, sure, we might be more motivated to do the ironing, but how often is that reward system going to happen? No, we need to find a better answer to the ironing challenge: motivation works a lot better when it is inside us and under our control. Every time we are dependent upon an external source for our motivation we weaken, we desensitize our own personal motivation.

Think carefully when you ask, "Why should I?" Every time we need someone to encourage or threaten us, every time we set up a carrot, we devolve our personal responsibility to external forces. And being organic we weaken a sensitive system. We all have a natural curiosity, a natural wish to deliver the goods. Notice the enthusiasm and curiosity of any healthy child. But if you observe children as they grow, these wonderful states tend to disappear in many cases. How and why? There are many reasons, of course, but unfortunately using and being in these states is not always rewarded. When they are in them, adult cynicism can knock children back. And children are increasingly expected to get used to the tough adult world.

Rediscover your curiosity and natural enthusiasm. Enthusiasm is a marvellous state: jobs are easier and more fun. People enjoy working with you. And you are a natural choice at any job interview.

Of course this is not saying you do not qualify suggestions or instructions, nor does it mean you don't seriously speak out when things need to be changed. But practice doing something, and doing something well, from your own resources. This is the transition to maturity, the fundamental evolutionary shift from child to adult, when we move from being dependent to being independent.

And, as I am sure you will have noticed, some never make that transition, that shift from dependence to independence. Instead they shift from the dependence upon a parent to undue dependence on the state or simply "them". "Them" being the unknown "they" who need to sort things out. Catch yourself saying "they". Who do you mean? The government? The board of directors where you work? Ask yourself what you are going to do, and if you feel "they" need to do something, how will you pursue that? Or drop it.

Remember always to ask: "What is in my control? What can I work on?" Address that rather than complaining about areas which are out of your control.

Here are the principles.

1. Of course it's great to be externally motivated, but incorrectly used it can desensitize our own personal motivation.

2. We strengthen our personal motivation by giving it attention, by using it.

3. We can choose to motivate ourselves by looking for the intrinsic worth of doing a job well. By firstly doing a job well for the pleasure of a happy customer and secondly for long-term skill development.

And one of the simplest ways of getting motivated is to start.

Craig really wanted to sort out the family finances. They were in a bad state. They had two incomes, the mortgage wasn't so bad and yet they were regularly overdrawn.

But he couldn't bear to start. He hated "finance stuff.". Detail. Cross-checking. Lists. Arithmetic. Budgets. Even the thought of these made him feel ill.

And yet it had to be done. He decided to wait until the weekend when he would be a little more relaxed. He sat down and started with a sigh, but an hour later the initial pain was over and he was making progress. Could he even dare admit that he was actually enjoying it?

Make a start: it's the best bet for getting motivated.

Here are the factors which will help you attain high levels of personal motivation.

1. **Whatever the task, look for its intrinsic worth.** In whatever the job or task, get used to finding the best. So you've regularly got to deal with the meanest boss in the world? OK, so let's see how quickly you can learn to manage them. You've been landed with this year's dreaded strategy report? How about if, thanks to your input, it was a useful document for once? Yes, sadly it's true that you may not get recognized for your efforts in your current role – but how about if you became so good at it that it became absolutely natural for you to make "excellence" your minimum standard? How many excellent people do you know around the place? Quite. Not many. Good news for you.

2. Realise that willpower consists of will (a decision) and appropriate power (an excellent state). Both of which you know how to achieve. Will is decision. State is MEDS. Practice taking decisions. Start with simple ones such as getting up at a certain time. Go on, try it. Or write down five issues which have been on your mind, for example:
- I think I want to change my bank.
- Should I start an Open University course?
- I need to go and see my sister in the USA.
- I need to sort my filing.
- Could I afford a holiday?

Now take a decision on each. And check out your state. It's very difficult to take balanced, energetic decisions when your state is poor.

3. Be absolutely clear on your vision (see V for Vision). This is your primary driving force. Is it on the wall, in your face? Is it up-to-date? Does it truly inspire you? Make sure.

4. Link to O for Organized. In particular:
- Break and date large tasks: they are often demotivating in their largest form.
- Always start a task. To wait until you are motivated is a poor strategy; you may never start.
- Be aware of continuing to "almost start" a task. It is possible to set up a condition, as with one of Pavlov's dogs. As you think about the task you simply don't want to do it. Break the pattern; do it in a different way.

5. Use your H for Hero mindset: be bigger than the pathetic task, be bigger than the pathetic in-tray.

6. **Remind yourself of what will happen if you don't achieve what you set out to do.**
   What will it cost you? Go on, write it down: The cost to me of not being sufficiently motivated
   to take a walk each lunch-time is:
   - I feel pathetic
   - I'm tired and never at my best
   - I'm going to continue to be overweight
   - If I can't even do this, how will I ever...

7. **Change your focus, your posture, your language.** Your focus is what you are thinking
   about. Are you worrying about what might go wrong or are you focused on possibilities? How
   are you sitting? Are you sitting at your desk as you would if you were to get some serious work
   done? Excellent. Are you talking problems or opportunities? Are you talking "they" or "I"? Are
   you talking "sometime" or "today"?

8. **Be grateful: write down your grateful list.** Start with something like this:
   - To be able to think about personal development.
   - To have health and to be able to improve it.
   - To have a brother even though he is a pain.
   - To be able to travel.
   - To be able to earn money.
   - To be able to help others.
   - To be able to get fresh fruit.

Brainstorm fifty. Add to the list. Regularly review it.

9. Return to simplicity. Write a simplicity list like this one and get rid of the "bugs" in your life.
- The Sunday papers: expensive, and trash anyway.
- My gym membership I don't use.
- Sugar-rich spreads from the cupboard.
- All the clothes I no longer wear.
- The piles of paper I intend to sort one day.
- Nine of my twelve credit cards.
- Three of the five televisions in the house.
- The old patio furniture.
- That pasta-making machine we never use.

Write your simplicity list, add to it every day and, of course, act upon it.

The greatest danger for most of us is not that our aim is too high and we miss it, but that it is too low and we reach it.
MICHELANGELO

"Motivation works a lot better when it is inside us and under our control."

N is Niche

Niche

When I say "Being the Best" I really mean Being the Best in your niche. We have to move away from the generic quest for success to the more specific one of being the best in a niche. The generic quest is likely to be difficult; there is simply a lot of competition out there. We can increase our chances and make it easier for ourselves by choosing our own specialist area. This links with all I have said to date and in essence is asking you to change appropriately; to simply be the best you can at what you do.

To become more successful more quickly, identify your niche: your own bit of the universe. Then you can really show off your expertise whether it be fudge making, asking precision questions or laying patios. To attempt to position yourself against the whole world is frankly futile; there are simply too many painters, too many novelists, too many carpenters, too many rock stars and too many accountants. (Although if you are reading this in the UK it is true that there are not enough good plumbers!) So, what's your specialty, your thing, your niche?

And yet it seems that those who truly want to be successful forget this basic fact. They think, "Heck, I've got to compete against that," by which they mean the brand name, of course. But who and/or what they are seeing are the high-profile niches such as professional footballing, rock stardom and the like. By far the majority of niches (including the fields of music, sport, business) are low-key, low-profile niches. But they are certainly ones in which you can gain significant recognition, earn plenty of money and perhaps more importantly have fun employing your skill.

So your niche is your specialist area, your area of expertise. Too many of us, in order to become successful, attempt to replicate the success of another person. It will work to a certain extent, but there comes a point when we need to innovate, to create breakthrough; to mark out our own area, to match to our own nature/nurture balance.

How do you identify your niche? Here are some ideas.

1. At work, which activities get you into a flow state? When do you get truly absorbed in what you are doing? When is your concentration so deep that if disturbed you can feel yourself surfacing? When do you not notice the flow of time? Is it when building a spreadsheet or resolving some issue of team morale? Or perhaps if you are honest, it simply doesn't occur at work. What about at home? When you are gardening or cooking?

2. If you could do anything and money were no object, what would you do (after you'd had the long holidays, moved house, etc)? Seriously consider this. It's a bit of a shock question for many. Assuming you have done the holidays, bought the Ferrari and so on, what would you do next? You have to be honest with this one. And maybe give it a bit of time. The thought of money being no object often sends us astray; we can't contemplate such a reality.

3. Is there a hobby or pastime you would love to extend? Think about this. Would you really want to play tennis all the time? So, no, that's probably not a good example. But do you love working with wood? Could you imagine doing that day in, day out? Making furniture? Making wooden toys perhaps? Does it give you a slight buzz (a positive physiological change, to use the jargon)? Then that's probably a very good sign.

Honest answers to those three questions are a good early indicator of your niche.

Always be clear by what you mean by success. In particular distinguish "success" from "profile," distinguish "success" from "money". Be clear what you mean. Be clear what you want.

Check out that your beliefs are truly supportive. As it dawns on you that your true passion is to be a breakfast show DJ, don't immediately stamp on it by saying to yourself "Of course, I'll never make that happen."

Once you have done as much work as you can on your own, there may be some "professional" work which you can do. An excellent investment is to discover your Myers Briggs profile (MBTI). The MBTI is a well-established, well-trusted psychometric indicator based upon the work of Jung. It will help you understand more about your true potential niches by encouraging you to think more about your preferences – the way you think and act. Some of us are much more time-and-deadline aware, for example. Some of us are happier accommodating conflict.

The MBTI has four scales. Here is a simple overview. Read it and if it appeals I would then encourage you to find a professional (try opp.co.uk) to administer the test and give you feedback. Do ensure your coach is accredited in the use of MBTI.

- **Scale 1** is the extroversion/introversion scale. Not solely about extroversion/introversion, this scale is an indicator of how we are energized: introverts can be more energized by their own thoughts, whereas extroverts often prefer discussion and the interaction of others.

- **Scale 2** is the sensing/intuition scale. Some of us prefer more practical "here and now" information (sensors). Others prefer to consider futures and possibilities.

- **Scale 3** is the thinking/feeling scale. This scale concerns how we prefer to go about making our decisions. Both thinkers and feelers like to be consistent. Thinkers prefer to be consistent to rules. Feelers prefer to be consistent to values.

■ **Scale 4** is the judging/perceiving scale, the "lifestyle" scale. Judgers prefer to have measures and know when thing are going to happen. Perceivers often prefer to leave things more fluid.

You will realise that the interaction of the four scales can give sixteen broad styles. Understanding your personal style can help with choice of niche, as you will have probably begun to detect already from this brief discussion.

To develop your niche you need some basic skills.

The skill of creating.

When we allow ourselves to be best in our niche, we are allowing ourselves to create. We are allowing ourselves to express. We are all artists at heart – whether it's in fudge making or patio laying. It's not just the painters and sculptors who can hang onto that title. It requires artistry to produce a superb meal, to develop a relationship, to design a garden. And it's a synergistic, iterative process: once you allow the artist in you to be released, it will be keen to express itself.

You will need to create on a regular basis. Whether it's software games or garden patios, or ways to manage your team, your audience is as fickle as ever. They'll be looking for what's new. And if you don't have something, they will go elsewhere. An important compass activity (and part of Compass Point I – career in C for Compass) is to be regularly reinventing and being creative. Will your niche allow you to do this? Even better, do you feel excited about it? These are excellent signs if you can answer in the positive.

Give careful balance to responding to customer needs and driving customer needs. An irony to be aware of is that if we remain too customer responsive, we may remove any innovation we have to offer.

The skill of selling
You may have a market, but will they buy? The answer is not necessarily. Individuals are so busy. So make it easy and uncomplicated to buy. Can you do that? Remember we are talking here both internally and externally. Be careful about being too sniffy about the business of selling.

The skill of prioritizing
You can only do so much in any one day. Don't burn out. Decide the priorities every year/every quarter/every month/every day. And stick to those. See O for Organized.

The skill of relating
Being successful is not just about a checklist. It's about emotions and people; particularly those who help you. Always return the compliment and remember to be a helper of others yourself. See E for Emotional Intelligence.

Over the years I have worked with a lot of event management companies. Here's one of them.

Ben's event management company was doing well. But not well enough. He was always under pressure from cash flow. He always seemed to be competing against "the big boys". And that presented him with a problem. If he did pitch against the larger companies, he wouldn't be able to match their capability. And if a client did choose him as opposed to one of the big boys, they were clearly attracted by his price, which put him under margin pressure.

Ben didn't normally have much respect for the bank, or for his business manager there, but this time he did have something useful to say. He asked Ben: "What's special about your business?" And Ben struggled – really struggled – to find an answer. He realised the manager had hit the key to his problems; his lack of niche.

Ben bought a marketing book, took a day off and created some true differentiation and identified his niche; the area in which he could become the best.

That day was a turning point. He never looked back; he became the best in his niche.

"Simply be the best you can at what you do."

O is Organized

How do you react to this one? Does it seem like the dullest of the A to Z? Are you looking forward to Z (Zen) and U (Uncertainty)? Does this letter seem so practical? So ordinary? Well, whatever you wish to achieve, you won't get it unless you are organized. No doubt about that.

Meg was an artist. It had taken her a long time to realise that. She'd started in marketing in a large pharmaceutical company, had then been headhunted and joined an agency. It had been fun, but she kept craving something. Eventually she decided that she needed more time for herself otherwise her creativity was stifled. So she left corporate life – her colleagues were staggered, but it was the best thing she ever did. The first six months were a joy. From her cottage in Wales she "remote-worked," selling her design concepts.

But then came month seven: crisis. Her bank manager wanted to know where the cash flow was. Meg couldn't believe she'd spent her savings so rapidly. Even with her ridiculously low mortgage she was having difficulty paying it. And she realised that hidden costs on her services were eroding her margin... She had to get organized. And she did. She set a timetable for her week: her "on" days; her "off" days. One afternoon was set aside for billing and paying checks. A two-day trip to London with a cheap stopover to meet her clients. A monthly mailshot. A definitive "master list" of plans, commitments and ideas; how had she managed to miss her mother's birthday?

Six months later the bank manager was congratulating her for her turnaround and improved turnover.

We all need to be organized: organization doesn't crush creativity; organization allows creativity.

You may be wonderful at designing things, but can you "organize" your purchases to save yourself money? And consequently keep your prices down? If you are consulting, are you sufficiently organized to maximize your billable time? Can you be organized with the taxman so that you don't need to endure uncomfortable and probing questions?

To become organized, consider a three-way approach.

Factor 1 is mental. You'll remember how important beliefs are in driving our behaviours and consequently our results? How do you think about organization? You don't?! Ah! Or if you do, is it with a feeling of resignation? Or desperation? How about if you changed that belief to be a belief of potential; a belief that when you are organized you can really show your potential, you can really release your abilities?

Factor 2 is management. How do you know which your priorities are, and which are the points you should be addressing? How do you project manage complex tasks?

Factor 3 is environment: your room, desk, lighting, etc. Your beliefs might be great, your systems wonderful, but if your working environment is poor, you'll certainly not be able to give of your best.

Let's examine each factor in turn.

Factor 1: mental

1. Decide that organization can only help you and that it doesn't require much organization to make the difference. Sometimes people say to me, "I bet Leonardo da Vinci wasn't that organized and yet look at everything he came up with." I reply "I think you'll be surprised." Visit his home town of Vinci near Florence in Italy and the two museums there, as I did.

2. Set your direction. The majority of people are driven by what is urgent; what is time and date stamped. But urgency is simply stuff which needs to be done now or as near to now as possible. It isn't necessarily important (meeting your goals). And, ironically, when things are urgent we don't get the time to consider them fully and do a "good" job. How can you urgently resolve a strategic crisis? How can you urgently set a new customer direction? How can you urgently build a new relationship with your teenage daughter? The answer of course is only to do it when it isn't urgent.

Doing tasks when they are important and non-urgent is choosing time which is important and investing. This sort of time is known as compass time, as you will know from C for Compass, as opposed to clock time which is important and urgent. Decide to choose compass time and not become ensnared in clock time. Realise that busy is not necessarily the same thing as productive and efficient is not necessarily the same thing as effective.

3. To ensure compass time is happening, schedule it. Two images may help you here. Firstly, a story which is often told is that of the rocks in the jar. Imagine an empty glass jar. Imagine a pile of fist-shaped rocks. How many of the large rocks can you get into the jar? Well, try and see. Maybe ten or twelve. The final number is not important. You'll notice that once you have filled the jar there is plenty of space around the big rocks. Here you can put smaller pebbles.

And around the smaller pebbles you can of course pack sand. And the sand will of course, absorb water. The story is reminding us that firstly we must know what is important – "the big rocks" – and secondly we must get them in to our schedule first before the rest of the other stuff which can so easily clog our lives. If we started with the sand and water and then added pebbles, some of the rocks would never fit in.

Secondly, do you remember the child's puzzle, the one where you have to move tiles around on a grid to create a picture? Typically there are eight tiles in a nine-square grid and one tile is missing to give you some room to manoeuvre, some slack. We, too, need to make sure that we have some slack for reflection, for manoeuvre in our lives.

Now, questions about what your "large rocks" should be and how much slack you should have are of course answered through the compass questions. You might want to review C for Compass.

Factor 2: management

Once you have decided what to do, then capture points on a master list. A master list is not a to-do list. Your Master List is a total overview of all that you need to do or want to do. It is kept in one place and is portable. At the end of each day we "break and date" our tasks; we break them into manageable components and then schedule them.

We work best when we are immersed in a task. Reduce interruptions as follows:

■ Choose environments which minimize interruptions.

■ Be assertive.

■ Don't make it easy for you to distract yourself or for people to distract you.

Here is a simple management structure.

■ Once a month, review the compass and capture points on your Master List.

■ Schedule the specific compass time per week. Ask how you are doing.

■ Daily: break and date, simplify and schedule.

■ Work tasks on a daily basis noting that slowly but surely they become compass tasks. Choose them by pay-off against your compass.

Factor 3: environment
Ensure that you have got a

■ clear working area

■ that it is well lit

■ that if lights and plants are important to you, they are present

■ that you have a plentiful supply of pens and pads.

Here is an implementation summary which brings in some points from some of the other letters and gathers them all in one place. You might try to attempt this over a five day period.

Day 1. Check your beliefs about organization, time and productivity. Try these:

■ I can choose my mental model of time.

■ I can manage my time, I simply need to give it attention.

■ I do this by choosing the correct kinds of task: important (meeting goals), investing (acting for the long term) and interesting (supporting my niche).

■ I deliberately do less to achieve more.

■ I am highly unlikely to be able to do everything I might wish in all areas of my life. And that's OK; I focus on the essential ones.

■ Above all, I shift my measure of productivity from what I do to a better one of what I achieve/create, to an even better one of who I am.

Day 2. Review what is important in your life; set your compass.

Day 3. Get your Master List up and running:

■ Get a hardback notebook

■ Write down all the things you need to do and want to do, at both home and work. Add any old lists. Have it all in one place. That night review it and decide the priorities for the following day. You could, of course, have this in an electronic format.

Day 4. Identify your "vital few" on your list: your very high pay-off items.

Day 5. What is distracting you? Create systems, like filing.

Get organized for results.

Structure
NATALIE GOLDBERG

P

P is Passion

Passion

Passion is more than motivation. Motivation is wanting to do what's necessary and being equipped to do it mentally and physically. However motivation can be "flexed". As we have seen, motivation can come externally. Motivation can be managed. Then there is passion: passion is something more; passion is an unstoppable force.

When we have passion we enjoy life, we have health, things get done, we ride waves of uncertainty with ease. What an amazing state! How about if it were available for you much more of the time?

Once you get passion, you can do anything, anywhere, anytime. Just get it. Passion we often associate with love, and you know what it does for you there:

Focus: I want him/her. I'll do anything to get him/her.
Clarity: He/she is all I can see.
Energy: I can make love all night and still have the energy I need for the next day.
Health: Colds just don't affect me.

How about if that level of energy were available to you for your work or your writing? It can be.

I was in a shop in London recently and I wanted the new Nick Hornby book; I couldn't see it anywhere. The assistant in the bookshop hunted high and low for the title I had requested, coping with a continual flow of interruptions as he moved across the floor. He loved books, he loved people and he did his job with energy and flair: he did it with passion.

On being asked where he got his enthusiasm from he said it was all about choice. And he had long ago learnt that things were a lot more fun when you did them with passion.

Here's the process. Passion is dependent upon:
1. Right focus.
2. Right state.
3. Right you.

Right focus

Are you truly being honest with yourself about your compass? Did you neglect the acting choice because of potential difficulties in finding a job on the stage? So, potentially, you chose a life-time of frustration compared to the occasional challenge of finding the next role? What does acting mean to you? Does it have to be the great Shakespearean part? Or how about becoming a soft-skills trainer?

One more time. Tackle your compass. Fully, honestly. No focus – no passion.
- **Career** – what do you want to do? How can you get started on that path?
- **Mind/body** – how can you take this to its next stage of development?
- **Finance** – boring isn't it? How can you get it sorted so you can realise true affluence?

- **Relationships** – which ones do you want? How can you develop them?
- **Fun** – make it mandatory!
- **Contribution** – start and you'll get your return.

Right state

Back to basics. Remember this? To develop passion you must have established the basics of essential energy. We summarize this in our MEDS routine:

M is meditating. Take time out. Invest in yourself. Practice meditation. Tai-chi, yoga...

E is exercise. Take regular cardio-vascular exercise. Release seratonin and endorphins to make you feel good.

D is for diet. Fuel in is results out. Eat the best fuels for energy.

S is sleep. Allow your body the quality rest it needs.

Right you

Seek authenticity. What on earth does that term mean? Authenticity is stopping pretending, it's being the real you. Start with the small stuff. If you really don't enjoy those dinner parties then stop going! If your job really isn't for you then think about a change. Being the real you is important. When you are not being you, you are constantly working against the grain, you are exhausting yourself. When you are authentic, the energy floods back. The state of passion is available.

Now would be a good time to take a break and really think about this one.

Whatever you do, do it with passion.
CARLOS CASTANEDA

Q is Quantum Leap

Quantum

Journalists use the word "quantum" to mean large. Physicists use it more accurately to mean "discrete", as when an electron moves from one shell to another in the atom – it makes a quantum leap. Interestingly, we don't see its passage between the two levels. This use of quantum certainly does not mean huge: relatively it's actually a tiny move. On our route to success we can make headway by making some "quantum" changes. These are changes that break barriers: changes that are both huge and discrete.

We don't need to use them all of the time, but occasionally we can make significant headway through a quantum change. Thus, in our quantum terminology, to launch your own restaurant business when previously you have been a trader on the money markets might be considered a quantum leap: a big step with no intermediate ones. A more traditional route might be to work for someone in the restaurant trade, gain experience, perhaps partner with someone who has successfully run a restaurant. Of course, the latter is a good route. But it has one big and one smaller disadvantage. The big one is that the process is very slow in the cumulative, iterative way. The other is that it doesn't necessarily increase your chances of success, although it feels that it ought to. One advantage of quantum thinking is that it gets you there quickly.

Let's begin in a small way with the classic nine-dot problem. No, please don't go. You'll not have looked at it this way before, I promise. Here's the problem:

● ● ●

● ● ●

● ● ●

Attempt to join all nine dots with just four straight lines. The lines must be continuously drawn without taking your pen off the paper.

Give up? Turn the page for the solution:

Don't complain. No one said you couldn't go outside the box. You put in that parameter which doesn't really exist. To get to the solution you had to think in a different way.

The point here is not the cleverness of the solution, but the fact that we needed to think in a totally different way to solve the problem. Many people, when shown the solution, miss the point that our original problem-solving technique simply wouldn't work until we set a different framework and, literally, thought outside the box.

When we do this we make a quantum leap: we get the best of the journalist's world (a large leap, i.e., great results) and the best of the physicist's world (a discrete solution, i.e., no in-between stages).

Here are some ways we have already seen Quantum Leap thinking in action:

1. Spending more time in compass time rather than clock time.

2. Realising that failure may well accompany success.

3. Investing in our state to help our practical behaviours.

4. Taking personal responsibility for our lifelong learning.

How about using it yourself? What about if you wanted to start your own business but kept worrying like this: "I need to support my family and can't if I start my own business." That's a point. How about if you made a Quantum Leap and said, "Now that I am running my own business I can support my family even better," instead?

Remember how in our compass point we made Quantum Leaps in our thinking?

Career – from a "job" to a true passion. We realise that the breakthrough here is nothing to do with a better job or more money or working harder – or even smarter (that's helpful, of course). The true quest is for our passion. What do we want to make our contribution to this amazing life be?

Mind/body – from simply being fit to total wellness. Our quantum breakthrough was to move from fitness, which is often controlling and a bit manic and which results in injuries, to a more holistic approach which considers our wellness.

Relationships – from "they" to "us". And to develop those that allow us to be authentic and alive.

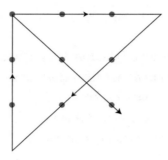

Finance – from wealthy to affluent, which moves from accumulation of "stuff" to true affluence. Affluence: an appreciation of what is available to us and how we might enjoy it.

Fun – from something special to "it's the norm".

Contribution – simply becoming a contributor.

So how do we become someone who makes more use of quantum thinking?

1. We must check our beliefs. We've spent some time on this already, but for example, watch out for ones like these:
  – I'm not creative...
  – I've never been good at solving lateral thinking problems.
  – I'm a bullet point kind of person.

Let's take each of these in turn.

"I'm not creative." Not true. Simply not true. You have a mental picture of creativity, I'm sure.

Maybe a potter or a mad scientist. But you're being creative already in reading this book: you are seeking to change and develop. And I'm sure that you are getting plenty of fresh ideas – and you'll get more as you let go of that label. How about a new belief? "Every day I get more creative."

"I've never been good at lateral thinking problems." Fine. They don't necessarily correlate well with true creativity and quantum thinking. They are convenient because they allow us to explain some concepts; nothing more, nothing less.

"I'm a bullet point kind of person." Good. We need those. How about if you bullet point your solutions to some problems, but just see if you can do it in fewer bullets?

2. Much of our thinking is, of course, revealed in our language. Watch out for these three patterns in your own:

Generalization
"I'll never be good at this stuff." This is, of course, a generalization. Decide to be good at it and stop generalizing. Generalizations are the basis of limiting beliefs.

Deletion
"I'm confused." OK, but what exactly are you confused about? Without precision you're going to stay confused.

Distortion
"My MBA tutor suggested I worked best in logical situations." OK, but that needn't stop you working in emotional situations.

3. Deliberately employ strategies to encourage your quantum thinking. These, in essence, will be encouraging your brain to work in a different way. This can be as simple as taking a break or getting a large sheet of paper to use in a brainstorming session. More sophisticated techniques can be found in the many good books on creative and lateral thinking; start with a study of Edward De Bono's work.

Many people manage to give up smoking having attended one of my workshops. Not because we specifically focus on that as an exercise, but because we focus on strategies for change.

Alfredo really wanted to stop smoking. In his home country it was still acceptable, but in his new American parent company, where he wanted to do well, it was certainly frowned upon. And he didn't want to die an early death due to smoking, like his father.

But it was hard. He was, he knew, addicted. He decided to do some quantum thinking. He isolated every benefit he got from smoking and listed them:
1. fulfils an addiction
2. allows me to stop/think/reflect
3. companionship
4. stress management
5. imagine my hero – silly as it might seem – Dirk Bogarde.

He took each of these in turn and radically broke the connection.

1. He loved good food and decided that whenever he thought about cigarettes he would think about and plan an excellent meal that he would make that evening. He would spend the money he saved on better food.

2. He discovered a local café where they didn't allow smoking. He took a pen and pad, and wrote while sipping his espresso.

3. He deliberately broke into a circle of non-smokers, one of whom encouraged him to use the gym.

4. He took up yoga and learned to meditate.

5. He decided to be his own hero – for giving up.

It took Alfredo seven months and two attempts. But now he feels he is a non-smoker.

Become a quantum thinker.

You can analyze the past, but you have to design the future.
EDWARD DE BONO

R is Rainmaker

Rainmaker

Can you make it rain? Can you influence? Can you sell? Can you become a marketer? Your route to success will require you to influence people's thinking and sell ideas. Perhaps your ultimate goal will require you to sell a product too. To get to where you want to get, you'll need support from those who agree, from those who differ, from those who are lethargic, from those who have lost the plot.

A rainmaker is someone who can make it happen. Someone who can get that level of support, who can get someone to think in another way.

Jon's biggest challenge: he couldn't make rain. Everything was everyone else's problem. "They should have done this!" "They should have done that!" "It's simply not possible."

After about twenty minutes of such language during a coaching session I asked Jon who "they" were.

"You know," he replied, "the senior people here."

"Who exactly?" I asked.

"Well, not so much a person. More the culture around here."

"But Jon," I insisted, "what makes a culture?"

All credit to Jon, he did agree that it was him as much as anyone else. At that moment Jon had the breakthrough he so desperately needed: to take personal responsibility. For himself, and for his life.

So how do you do it? How do you become a rainmaker? Here are 17 ideas.

Idea 1. Don't become a "technique" person. The business of selling has been all but destroyed by techniques. Is there a need for your idea or product or service? Can you create a need for what you are offering?

If so, that's fine. If you know there's a need or if you can create a need then you can be a rainmaker. Use your lifelong learning principles and your team to get close to real marketers and effective salespeople.

Idea 2. Stay human. When people start selling, something too often happens to them. They think they have to be "closing" all the time or chanting "benefits" continuously. There's no need for that. Have normal conversations with people in normal ways. But given that you are influencing someone's thinking, pay particular attention to everything which might influence them. Such as the following ideas!

Idea 3. The way you communicate. Different people communicate in different ways. Notice whether the person you are trying to influence is more visual, in which case it might help if you used the whiteboard a little more or drew some outlines on your pad. Maybe they're more practical, "hands on" people. Then some real examples could help them, or you could show them how your product/service would work or you could take them to a current customer. Maybe they like to talk things through and explain back ideas. Whatever their preference, help them understand by communicating in their way as much as possible.

Idea 4. Talk benefits. Benefits are reasons for wanting to proceed with your idea. Benefits come in different forms; some are just pure solution reasons – they fix a problem. Some are financial reasons – save money or make more money. Some are emotional reasons – attractiveness of design or "everyone else has one".

Think about the role of the person you are trying to influence. Decide what kind of benefits would be of most interest to them. Remember that even the most logical of decision makers will still make decisions for emotional reasons.

Idea 5. Remember that a valid reason means it would be good to "buy" your product or idea sometime; it doesn't mean it would be a good idea to buy it now. Nor does it necessarily (now that you have opened up to such an awareness) mean that your solution will be seen as the definitive one.

Help your decision maker understand why your solution is the best one and why they need to take action now. Why are you the best person for the job and why are you ready now? Why should the bank give you that loan and why should it be willing to give you additionally favourable terms?

Idea 6. Do the basics: dress appropriately. Be wary of dressing down too much. Have a notebook. Take notes; not too many, but the essentials. Arrive on time and always set a follow-up date before leaving.

Idea 7. Get better and better at giving quantitative reasons, especially if you are hoping to make a big sale. Can you show a ROI – a return on investment? You might get current clients to help you with the figures. If you are trying to get a new job, show the return you would expect to make for the organization. Illustrate the costs of delay.

Idea 8. Ask those you influence for help in influencing others. Ask them who they would go to see. Ask them which of your arguments impressed them the most (you may well be surprised).

Idea 9. Structure your conversation. Think about the different types of questions you might ask.
- Open – to encourage conversation: for example, "What is your strategy on this project?"
- Closed – to get a definitive, finite response, especially yes or no: "So you will be the team leader?"
- Agreement – to decide what happens next: "So the next stage is...?"
- Implication – to cause your decision maker to reflect on an issue: "What would that mean for your cost base?"

Idea 10. Build personal relationships; be courteous and do what you say you will do.

Idea 11. Build networks: build up a network of business contacts.

Idea 12. Get to the highest decision maker possible, and stay as high as possible for as long as possible, by creating valid reasons for them to see you.

Idea 13. Build a range of opportunities. Think of your sales as being in a funnel; you will probably lose some along the way.

Idea 14. Being a rainmaker includes the skills of both sales and marketing. They are simply different emphases on the same business. When marketing, keep it practical and look for results.

Idea 15. Package all your ideas so that you have them in one place and can easily refer to them at any time in the discussion.

Idea 16. Do not expect it to be an easy "yes". You have been living and breathing this pet project of yours for a long time. You are intimate with every detail of it; no wonder you are confident. No wonder you feel it is stupid of someone not to want to go ahead. But you need to get inside that decision maker's head and realise that they are new to your idea.

Idea 17. Decide to become a rainmaker. If you consider the business of selling and marketing – especially selling – below you, then the rains won't come.

You are only as good as your last gig.
TOM PETERS

S is Success

Success

AHA! The big one! I have, of course, referred to "success" in almost every letter. After all, that is why we are studying the A to Z. But the time has come to get precise. So, what is success? Well, ultimately that is for you decide. A certain job, an achievement. A level of wealth or health, or both. Or love, or a family. Or all of those, or none of those. But one thing is certain, it is not necessarily – and need not be at all – fame and riches. And many find, when they do choose the fame and riches route, that it is not that much fun when they get there.

The big learning curve for many is that it's not necessarily money itself that we desire, it's rather what the money can buy. This may be toys, houses or the ability to have freedom and choices. And for those latter qualities you don't need to be rich and famous; in fact, you will be well aware that you shouldn't become rich and famous if you genuinely crave freedom, simplicity and the ability to make choices. So think carefully because if you start giving attention to it, you'll find it starts happening!

What's the approach? Something along these lines.

1. You are successful already.

Whatever you are currently doing, even if you have recently been made redundant, realise and focus on what you are already successful at. Yes, you will, of course, want more, because humans are motivated by growth and challenge; so simply work at being an even better example of you. It is natural for you to want success. And it is also true that there are some things you would like to change. Maybe you simply wish you didn't have to commute so far or perhaps you want some spare cash instead of really struggling at the end of each month.

2. Be careful that you are not restricted by society's message of what success is.

This can lead you up the wrong path. Truly decide, through reflection, what success is for you. And think deeply behind the desire. To be a director of your organization? Exactly why? Status? When I am doing coaching I find the biggest challenge is that individuals have often become so heavily committed to status that they have lost the plot about what is really important.

3. Success is not a straightforward path.

You'll know already from your studies of the other characteristics that we must give it attention. The final subtlety is to understand the success curve:

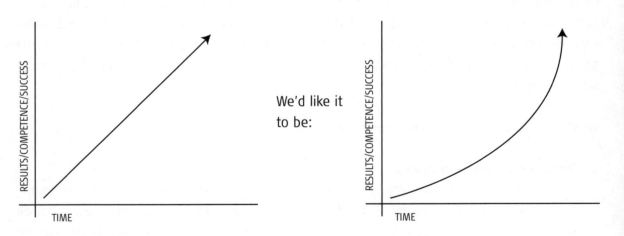

We'd like it to be:

In fact it's not a nice linear graph. It's true that we will always be getting results, but some of these results will take us away from success; they're our failures.

Specifically, the success curve can look more like this:

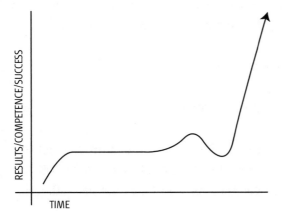

You'll notice two practical features: one is the plateau. A plateau is where we notice that things don't seem to be improving. And it is just as true of our tennis back-hand as it is of our business development. Despite working at something, it gets no better. That's because we have just made some huge changes and we are going through a period of consolidation.

Sometimes, things appear to get worse and our ability drops; we go into a fall. This is a process of rewiring. And it may be at a micro level within our own head, or at a macro level within an organization.

Here's an important message. Celebrate each plateau, celebrate the falls. They are on the way to something greater!

Let's summarize:

1. Success is what you want. But your definition of success is likely to include growth, connection and freedom and less likely to be money and stuff. Money and stuff is only the measure.

2. Success will arrive, but along the way expect plateaus and falls.

3. This is true of anyone who has ever got the success they wanted.

Roger Bannister, who ran the first sub-four-minute mile in 1954, came fourth in the Helsinki Olympics in 1952; the Beatles played for three years in Hamburg before returning to the UK and acclaim. Howard Schultz was turned down for venture capital over 200 times before getting his Starbucks vision to come to reality.

Here are some rather more personal examples.

Plateaus
- **Juggling**: Expect to drop the balls. When you learn to juggle two balls you'll drop the third. When you can juggle three balls, try four. Guess what? But learning to juggle equals dropping balls. The more you drop balls, the sooner you'll have got the juggling going.

- **Learning a language**: Why does the adjective generally go after the noun in Spanish? If you've not learned a similar language you'll find it so tricky; it's easy to get it wrong. Then suddenly you've got it and you're at the next stage. You've been on the plateau.

- **Leading**: You've found you can lead some, but not all, of your team. If you are a parent you're working well with one of your children, but not with another. And then it will switch.

Falls
- **Personal development:** At times you feel great. At other times you feel sad, realising how little you know.

- **Health:** As you detox you seem to get worse. And worse! You come off smoking and you get fat. You come off dairy, and get acne. You come off sugar, and you are irritable.

Here's one many of us have experienced. How did you cope?

Ruth was pretty fed up; she'd delayed taking her driving test until she started university partly because she had wanted to concentrate on her school examinations, and partly because she hadn't been able to afford it before. But now she'd got to university and she'd failed her test twice. The theory test had been easy, of course, and she realised that theory always was for her. It was the practical test that caused the problem. She was almost ready to give up in despair, and the only thing that made her feel better was that she wasn't the only one; plenty of other people seemed to fail too.

Then one evening at her judo class she got a message: while you are learning a new skill there will be plateaus when you appear to be making no progress, and dips when you seem to have to re-learn a skill you thought you had mastered. Her judo instructor reminded the class that the dips and plateaus were normal and they needed to go through them to excel.

With this new mindset Ruth approached her driving lessons with more determination and confidence. The next time she took her test, she passed.

That's the reality: dips and plateaus.

Things will not always go to plan. As children we fell off our bikes again and again when learning to ride. Clearly, that wasn't failure; it was feedback that we needed to practice more, to develop our balance. And as children we are normally good at understanding that process. But something happens as we become adults; we reach a very dangerous state called "cool". In the state of cool we won't do anything unless we can do it perfectly. Oh dear, dangerous...

Celebrate the plateau. Celebrate the fall. They are normal, to be accepted on the way to something greater.

Love the dip and love the plateau.
GEORGE LEONARD

"So, what is success? Well, ultimately that is for you decide."

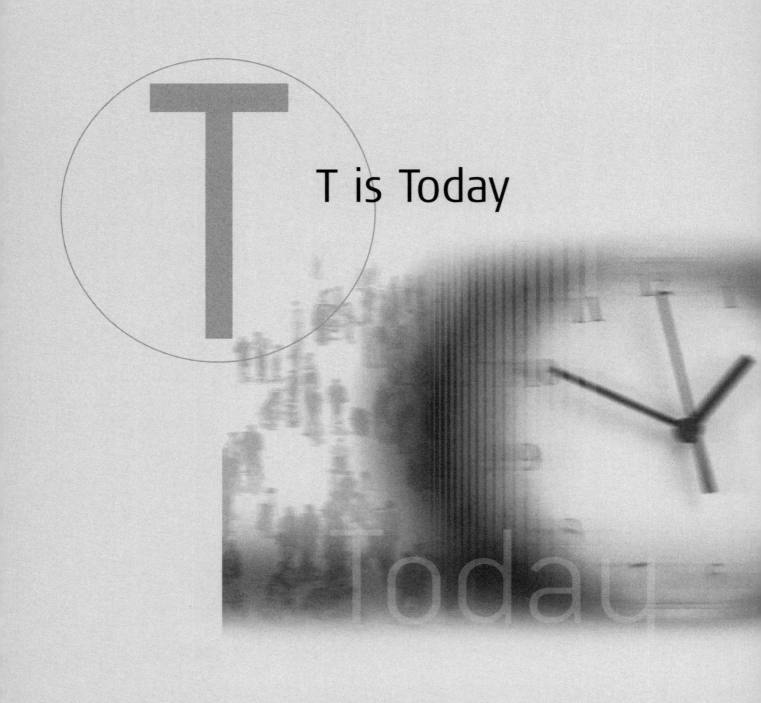

T is Today

Today is a really good time to start making the changes you seek and creating the successes you want.

You see, tomorrow never comes. The language of tomorrow too often means no real action. The language of tomorrow too often is procrastination. "Tomorrow" is another reason why nothing is done today. However, the language of today means:

- No further excuses.
- Start.
- No more planning.
- Today is the day.
- The delight of progress.
- The buzz of success.

Today thinking might be seen as being at odds with much of what we have been talking about. Our emphasis has been to stress planning, vision, strategy, goals. However it has also been very much to stress attention. And attention is something we do *now*.

Once you can regularly act for today, you are ready to live for today. We have seen how easy it is to talk of actions that we will do sometime, and we have seen strategies for overcoming that. Here we are going on to the next stage, the stage of living for today. Living for tomorrow is focused on how things will be better in the future. And, yes, they will be. But they will be particularly better when we become good at living in today and for today.

How do we live for today?

1. Get more specific. Focus on one thing at a time and give it 100 percent attention. Don't hold conversations while thinking about something else. Leave aside all the things that are troubling you, worrying you at the moment. If you do have things that are worrying you, then decide to address them and do address them; then get back to today. Many people at work long for home and their down time. Many people, while at home and "relaxing," worry about work. Notice what is great around you. The weather? Environment? Opportunities? Having trouble? Then what about you? Fit and well?

Today is the day; now is the time to start! There is no better time to begin work on the significant changes that you want to see. Today is "pebble in the pond" day; notice the ripples. Start the changes today that will create the life you will start living in just a few months from now. You have prevaricated and procrastinated, you've discussed and networked, you've read the books and listened to the tapes. You even went to the States and went on the original course. You could do more preparation, of course. We can always do more to make sure that we are absolutely ready. But leave that for the future. Start work with what you know now. Now.

2. Focus on today's actions. Don't be forever planning tomorrow. What are you about today? What are you attempting to be today? Write them down, now. Are you using your Master List (see O for Organized) on a regular basis? If not, make that something to start immediately.

3. Create rituals that allow you to engage with the day. By "rituals" I mean something that you always do which always engages you. Great rituals are:
- Early morning and early evening meditations.
- A quiet reflection with a hot drink.

- A solo lunchtime walk.
- Doing some writing in a café.
- Making a date with yourself; fix a day for going to an art gallery or museum.
- Getting together with a close friend or a long-lost school mate, perhaps from Friends Reunited. No, I know it's not the sort of thing you usually do. But it will ground you.
- Writing in your journal.

You could also create three points during the day – perhaps 7 a.m., 12 noon, 7 p.m. – when you stop for five minutes and re-engage.

4. Try the following fun exercise. As you walk to work, practice describing what you see. Take this to a greater level of detail than you normally would. For instance if you notice a car driving too fast, ask yourself what kind of car it was and what speed you thought it was going. Who was driving it? Were there any passengers? Try observing some buildings. What textures are attractive to you?

Enough is enough. Let's live and breathe this letter. Today is the day to start.

No excuses, now. Turn to your schedule, wherever you keep it. Create a one-hour piece of time solely dedicated to you. Today or tomorrow or at the very latest, the following day. Yes, you can. Something will move. You can't procrastinate any longer.

I know that it feels difficult. There are many reasons, but they certainly include the practical issue of squeezing time and the emotional feeling about taking time for yourself. But put these problems aside. Find that one hour. Know that if I were there I would find that time for you.

Take your notebook for that one hour. Don't miss it. Don't shorten it, do rationalize. Keep it as intended: one hour of dedicated time.

Now we get to the crucial part. When your designated hour arrives, firstly stop. Breathe normally. Slow down. Break from whatever you were doing previously. Pick up your notebook and pencil. Write clearly on the pad: "This one hour is about me and the changes I need to make." Don't use the time for thinking about anything else. Go for a walk, walk briskly and think. At the half-way point, say after twenty minutes, stop and write fast. These are the things that you must do immediately to get the changes you need. Write seven actions. No more, no less. Now put them in priority order: the most fundamental and important first. Now put a day of the week alongside each of the actions.

Then transfer each action to its own page, one per page.

And now on each page, answer these important questions:
1. What exactly is the action? Is it absolutely clear?
2. What do I need to do first?
3. What will I gain by taking this action?
4. What is the cost if I don't take this action this week?

Here is an example with particular reference to "today".

Restoring work/life balance

Seven areas identified:

1. Go home on time three out of five nights
2. Never use laptop or email at home
3. Help children with reading
4. Take Lucy to club on Wednesday
5. Make Fri/Sat our night
6. Find decent babysitter
7. Start reading about work/life balance tips

Action 1. Go home on time three of five nights: task allocated to Monday

Exactly what is the action? Leave building at 5.45 p.m. on Mon, Wed, Thurs
What must I do first? Get manager's support
What will I gain when I do it? Sanity/time/family life
What will I lose if I don't do it? Most important thing to me: family

Now, walk back feeling very different. Start. No excuses. You've done those. You are a different person, now. From now on today will always be a day of action for you. It will never be tomorrow.

I run a two day personal development workshop called "Personal Excellence". It's designed to allow individuals to release and realise their true potential. As we work together I push for decisions and actions. I respect the differing natures of individuals and the need for some to reflect before they act, but I still encourage action and decisions. "So what will you do?" I ask. "And how will you do it? By when?"

A great surprise for many of the course participants is that at the end of the first day I ask for some actions which they will take away and work on *that evening, even though there is a further day to go.* Why? Because I want to encourage them to live and breathe the material, to start making changes. To become somebody who does what they say they will do.

I encourage them to challenge their belief about busyness and difficulties, and just do it. And do you know what? The majority do; and they are very pleased with themselves. Suddenly they have become change agents.

Life is what happens to you while you are busy making other plans.
JOHN LENNON

"Today is a really good time to start making the changes you seek..."

U is Uncertainty

A breakthrough on your path to success will be when you are able to accept uncertainty.

This guide book – the A to Z – will undoubtedly increase your chances of success. But nothing's certain. For those of us who love clarity, like definition, and need to know, the quest for more certainty can frustratingly lead to more uncertainty. And the desire to remove uncertainty can eliminate some of our biggest opportunities for success.

Take any subject, and success is no different. As we gain in expertise, we realise how little is truly certain; we discover that atoms are not at all like solid billiard balls as we had been initially led to believe. That the French actually don't use that particular past tense in actual conversation, and that the coastline's length simply gets longer the more precisely you attempt to measure it. It was true at school and college when we got to the periphery of a subject. And it's true in life as we gain in wisdom and expertise; the answers aren't clear nor, in fact, are the answers as robust as we originally thought.

For example, maybe you want to be successful in improving your health; you've had some chronic difficulty. You have discovered that no one is definitely sure how to solve that heart problem. Some suggest surgery, some powerful drugs, some meditation, some all three. What do you do? You accept that you can't know definitely. You research, you learn and you follow your intuition. It is not a sign of weakness to be uncertain, as long as we are aware of that and apply our intelligence appropriately. And what is more dramatically true for health is true in our personal lives, our relationships and our job security.

Notice how consistently politicians let us down through their inability to tell us they are uncertain and by an insistence that they have an answer when they clearly have not. Equally we kid ourselves that we feel we know when we don't. It's an uncertain world out there: from pensions to weather patterns to international tensions.

If you insist on seeking certainty in everything you do, you may feel and experience constant and regular frustration as you try and pin down that which is not to be pinned down. Equally you miss out on a fast track to your success.

Well, we will, if we follow the A to Z guidelines, undoubtedly eventually get what we want:

- An early retirement.

- A Ferrari.

- Getting that book published.

- Fluency in Spanish.

- A landscaped garden.

- A holiday home in Scotland.

We will accomplish it. But not maybe in the way we set out to do; we'll find retirement is not as we expected, the Ferrari is a nuisance around town. And we'll be uncertain what to do next. This is a good time to go with the flow a little more – just to see what happens, not to try to get everything to fit our plan.

So, learn to love uncertainty. Why? Here are a few good reasons.

1. **Your certainty path is just one path: just one way of doing things.** There's undoubtedly a lot of exciting stuff on that plan. But there are an infinite number of uncertainty paths, too. These are also very exciting. Now, clearly, I am not saying follow them all. But if you happen to stumble on one of them, who knows what might emerge?

2. **Uncertainty is fun whenever you are in a receptive mood.** You know what it's like: say that on a recent trip to Seville you forgot the guide book, headed for the old town and got a bit lost. But you did find some places you'd have never come across otherwise. And you got much more opportunity to use your Spanish. It was fun.

   Or at work, you took that project which no one else wanted. You were damn uncertain about its potential. But you applied what you had learned to be as an A to Z thinker; it worked out and funnily enough you got more credit than you would have done had it been a sure-fire winner.

3. **Uncertainty gives you access to creative breakthroughs.** Whatever your role, whatever your job, you will appreciate that creativity. However, it can be so easily quashed by a desire for certainty, so what's the best way to think of some alternatives? Just think of some alternatives. "What if?" thinking is only powerful when it springs out of curiosity rather than fear.

4. **Uncertainty can be an easy route into what some of those who are successful see as some of the higher but often ignored forces which are available to us.** Allowing uncertainty into your life often allows other associated forces in too. And you don't necessarily

need to believe in these. Just notice the results. What if there were some higher force which supported us when we relaxed a bit? I said that you don't need to believe this. But it is making you a little uncertain, isn't it? Just allow them to work.

A force many successful people often talk about is luck. And most will say, "You make your own luck." Luck is preparation, planning and opportunity coming together. But relaxation is often about sensitivity and getting receptive.

5. Uncertainty will allow you to develop those qualities which will reinforce your emotional intelligence:
  – Acceptance: an ability to simply accept what is happening and live with it. Fighting everything reduces your energy output. So they screwed up and won't sort it out – move on and don't use them again.

  – Openness: an ability not to argue in the case of a divergence of opinion, but listen to it, explore it and see how it goes.

  – Self-awareness.

6. Uncertainty is not silly. As we measure and metric and litigate the spontaneity out of the world, realise that uncertainty is not foolish but remarkably powerful. Can you be uncertain enough to cope?

So how can we develop our "uncertainty ability"? Also, how do we balance certainty against uncertainty?

- Resist the temptation to judge rapidly. Be willing to suspend your judgment of others and of situations. Hang on in there before closing down your decisions; see how it works for you.

- Practice developing physical and mental skills which leave you exposed to uncertainty: physical ones such as juggling, mental ones such as attempting to memorize quotations. Notice the feeling in your body.

- Read beyond your main subject, especially if your subject is one which is "certain". Try reading about Zen, or the outer reaches of the universe, or quantum mechanics or chaos theory.

- Give yourself a couple of hours off and decide to travel. By foot or bus or car. Don't plan. And allow yourself to make last-minute decisions. Where did you end up?

Certain versus uncertain.

People like to ask when they should act "certainly" and when "uncertainly". Well, guess what? There's no easy answer. But as you think carefully about it, perhaps you learn that certain is simply a special case of uncertainty. And that's all we are aiming for occasionally. At times things come together and we can plan around that.

But deep down, we can never be certain about our job, our relationships, our pension. So learn to love uncertainty.

He'd been very awkward from the moment the program started; asking difficult questions and not accepting anything initially.

I've always had a belief that all delegates will get there eventually, it's just that some take a little longer than others. And I must admit that this one was really causing me a great deal of uncertainty. Should I ask him to leave? Have a one to one discussion? Or just wait to see how it would go?

Fortunately it was a period when I was trying to explore the whole business of uncertainty, so I just decided to see where our currently challenging relationship went.

I have to admit it was tense at times. But to cut a long story short, we did develop a great working relationship. He caused me to tighten up a lot of my thinking and teaching, and he introduced me, with a glowing recommendation, to what was to become one of our most important accounts.

"The desire to remove uncertainty can eliminate some of our biggest opportunities for success."

V is Vision

Vision

Towards the end of World War II an American Dakota plane came in over the Scottish Isle of Mull and, in heavy fog, crashed into Beinn Talaidh, one of the tallest mountains in the area. A dramatic rescue was staged by locals and, although there had been casualties, the survivors were brought down to safety. The wrecked plane was blown up and the remains pushed into a river gully.

Some 50 years later a young boy visiting the museum in Tobermory on Mull was captivated by this story and by the buckled piece of aluminium displayed there; part of the wing of the Dakota. Could there be any more bits of plane to be found on the mountain? He asked at the museum. No, came the reply. All gone long ago, said the locals. Very unlikely, said his parents.

But the boy continued to dream and to plan. He was convinced that if he climbed the mountain he would be able to find the site and pick up a part of the plane. He studied the maps and identified the river gully. The following year, when the family returned to the island, he insisted that they climb the mountain. His parents tried to prepare him for disappointment but he didn't waver in his certainty that he would find what he was looking for.

The weather was cold and wet, the climb tiring. Near the summit the rest of the family were ready to give up, but the boy encouraged them to go just a little further, toward the gully where he had judged the plane would have ended up. As they made their way, exhausted, following the river, he saw it; a small scrap of aluminium. And then another, and another. Saying a prayer, they took a souvenir – of a plane's brave flight, and a young boy's vision.

Vision makes things happen.

I know that you will enjoy this characteristic. One of the things that you will know about those who are successful and who get things done is that they have a vision. Here's a chance to get some clarity on your own particular vision.

Take an A4 sheet of paper and a couple of coloured pens. With the paper landscape, rather than portrait, draw. What? Ah – your vision. How you want things to be in three years time. Don't allow any limiting beliefs to sneak in. And remember how you want things to be. Not how you are convinced they will be at the moment. Just what you want things to be like. Draw and please do it now; when you have finished, come back to these notes. Just work. There's no rush. And having just covered uncertainty, we can approach this exercise with that mindset. Have no judgment of your artistic ability, have a child-like enjoyment of the process of drawing. Use plenty of colour, texture, thin and thick pens. Let go. See what happens.

How did it go? What happened? Did any parts surprise you? Is there more work? Or less work? Or what? Here are some facets of your vision that you may wish to explore. But please be aware there are no right answers. These are simply points to think about.

What was central to your vision?
These will be the areas which are most important to you. There may have been one or two, or several. It may surprise you what develops there. Equally you may realise that there are one or two other elements which you would like to be central. In which case, draw them in – if that's what you want. Not just because you feel you ought or should. Watch out with these latter words. When you sense them popping into your head ask, "According to whom?"

What did you draw first?

What went down on the paper? Was it the big goal you have had since childhood? Was it family, friends, your new...?

Was there a greater focus on work or home?

Did that surprise you? When we are given a free hand to express a vision it is often a shock to discover how little attention we have given to our work. Maybe a totally new aspect of your work came into your drawing? How much was your unconscious brain working there? Something to think about...

What were the connections? Or what were the discrete parts of your picture?

How did it appear? A montage, a great panorama or discrete, boxed chunks? Did pieces appear to be missing? And had you connected them? How? Overlapped as Venn diagrams? Or as lines, and were they broken or complete?

What were the flashes of inspiration?

What aspect were you particularly pleased about? Your flashes of inspiration? What just arrived, came out of nowhere as your pen moved across the paper?

Were there any breakthroughs? Were there any surprises?

I'm in the wrong job! I miss my son! I want to write a novel!

If you did manage to let go, your unconscious thinking may well have thrown up some interesting emphases. For now, decide three specific things that you could do to pursue your vision and make it more likely to happen.

And if you feel a little frustrated with your vision, leave it for a day or two and then start again, afresh. Perhaps you simply need to loosen up a little.

When you feel happy with the drawing of your vision, frame it and consider it every day. But note: if you are tempted to get it professionally drawn, make sure the artist does not reinterpret the nuances of your picture.

Dream as if you'll live forever. Live as if you'll die today.
JAMES DEAN

"Vision makes
things happen."

W is Who

W is Who? You can't do it all on your own. Well, you can, of course. But why do so? "Who" is encouraging you to enlist the help of others. It'll speed up the process and development of your skills and be fun. You need a team. And the good news is there's an extensive team of people out there who can help you.

By this stage you should be very clear on what you want. The question now is who can help you achieve it? Here are the possibilities.

Who is in your real learning team?

By real learning team I mean those people who you have teamed up with in order to spend one hour per month working in a highly dedicated manner on your learning. (see L for Lifelong Learning). In the dedicated hour you will share learning from books, tapes, experiences. You will learn things from your colleagues who will do the same for you. You will network and share rolodex contacts. In this dedicated hour there will be absolutely no social grease at all. It will be a dedicated hour of learning. Possible activities are:

■ Sharing an aspect of learning since your last meeting.

■ Sharing a success or breakthrough in your current project.

■ The biggest challenge you are currently facing.

■ The types of people you find challenging – how do others in your learning team manage them?

■ Doing some collective work on improving note-taking and reading skills.

■ Sharing one insightful anecdote.

■ Sharing a physical skill such as juggling, a technique for finely chopping an onion, etc.

Whom should you choose?
The most important characteristic is undoubtedly someone who is as dedicated to the business of learning as you are – someone who will turn up, who will do their homework, who will never be late and who can do without fifteen minutes of whinging every time. Then seek out those who will stretch you, not necessarily those who are comfortable with you.

Who do you spend time with?
Who are your social contacts? Are you having fun with them? If so, great. If not, then decide to spend less time with anyone who is deliberately unsupportive or negative. Are you worried about making such a change? Will people think that you have become aloof? Is it that you like their company anyway, but you'd just like some variety? Read I for Internally-referenced, and go ahead and do it.

Who is in your virtual team?
Your virtual team works only in your mind but, of course, don't underestimate the power of that. The individuals in it can be living or dead, but the important thing is that you can call on them at any time (mentally, if need be) and ask the powerful question: "if you were here, what advice would you give me?" Who can give your neural network a jolt in another direction? Start with the people who come immediately to mind, but then expand. Make sure that you include or consider:

- Your family: what did your mother always used to say?

- Your schoolteachers: which teacher was the most inspiring?

- College lecturers: who got you into that "can do" mentality?

- Early career managers: who stuck their neck out for you?

- Figures from history: did some of those early scientists impress you with their dedication?

- Figures from fiction or drama.

Who and what are you reading?

Who's written a book, just one page of which may well give you the answer and/or inspiration you were looking for? Browse on Amazon. Perhaps go outside your main area. Think of a surname. Search and see what books are available by that person, get one and read it. Try a bit of synchronicity.

Who has been your greatest inspiration?

Why? Do you know any others like them? Could you read about them?

So, just to be clear. You must know what you want or your best guess at what you want. Then:

1. Given that some skills, talents and attitudes are missing, who could help you? Who could you ring or email? Ensure that you think about who might be a help, not just about who is nice or friendly. Do add authors of those books which you have found helpful.

2. Put their names in order of priority. And email to arrange a ten-minute call.

3. If they say no, realise that they mean no – for today.

4. Get very focused with your questions; don't waste their time.

5. Always thank them for their help. Keep a simple rolodex of your contacts.

Your network will be able to help you in many ways:

■ As a resource. Perhaps someone in your family can help you with your business start-up until cash starts to come in.

■ As validators: bounce ideas off them. What do they think?

■ As encouragers/inspirers. Try hard to spend time with like-minded people. These will encourage you with your ideas and inspire you. So many people have done great things because they were encouraged at the right time by the right people.

■ As information sources. These are particularly useful where you may be using external experts.

■ As standards experts. Attempt to spend time with those who have the highest of standards; they'll remind you if you are aiming high enough.

When you are asking questions, frame them carefully. What exactly do you want to know? Get precision. So often people will say to me: "I asked the expert but they wouldn't give me the information I needed." That's probably because the correct question wasn't asked.

Rather than asking "How do you stay motivated?" try something like "How do you pick yourself up after losing a match?" Instead of "How do you present to large groups?" try "Do you have a tip for the opening minutes of an important presentation?"

And do not forget to return the compliment. Help and support other people as well, and as much, as you can. Be careful about giving away too much of your time, but do be responsive. Say "Sure, if you'd like to email me two questions in advance I'll certainly do my best."

Occasionally you'll come across one of those rare opportunities to ask some specific questions of one of your role models. Key areas to cover are:

■ What motivates them, especially when they are down.

■ Where they get their learning from.

■ Who their role models are.

■ What tips would they give you?

■ What they are currently reading.

■ Might they be able to introduce you to any of their network?

When Paul was made redundant he went through the normal stages. (He could see himself doing it.) He fought it for a while. Then he accepted it. Then he got lazy and did nothing. And waited.

But four months later he was still waiting and market conditions were tougher than ever. It was time for action. On a fresh pad of paper he wrote the name of every friend or contact that he could think of from school, college and his work to date. Everybody. He logged on to Friends Reunited. He came up with a list of 175 people, some close friends, some remote contacts. He composed three letters depending on how well he knew the recipient. He was clear about the reason he was contacting them: he needed a job and he would consider almost anything.

He sent them off, emailing wherever possible. Of the 175:
86 didn't reply
17 rang for a chat
12 suggested meeting
22 apologized, but couldn't help
16 had ideas
22 had real offers.
Of the 22 real offers, six were worth considering and two were really exciting. He took the best offer.

Help yourself to ask who can help.

And in the end, the love you take is equal to the love you make.
LENNON and McCARTNEY

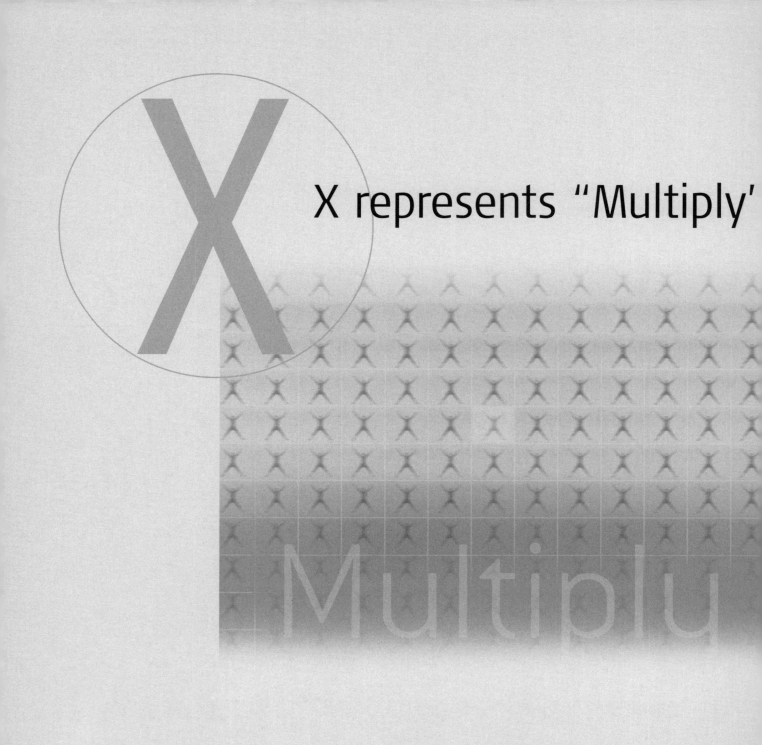

X represents "Multiply"

We significantly increase our chances of success when we bring together a collection of the A to Z success characteristics. Consider the impact, for example, of not only giving the area you wish to develop attention, but also of working on any limiting beliefs which you might have while at the same time you developed a hero state of mind.

We could represent this as:

Attention x belief x hero.

Clearly through this we get a cumulative effect. When making changes, string together as many of the factors as you can and attempt them at the same time. Often, when we work on the changes that we wish to make we hit on just one factor. Perhaps because that is where we went wrong previously or we've read a book on that aspect or... But it's rarely a factor. It's a story.

Take A, attention. That's good. But attention to what? Ah, that's C, compass. OK, but what about working with people? Ah, that's E, emotional intelligence.

But if we were being picky, isn't this strictly just addition? Doing one factor, then another factor, then... No, the factors are synergistic. Applying two factors gives considerably more power than the sum of the two factors on their own. This is because we separate the factors for ease of understanding; but of course in reality we must connect the different factors. Applying a new factor gives us greater realisation and hindsight into an earlier factor.

How do we multiply?

Choose any one factor; apply it to the best of your ability. Then just when you feel you have exhausted your study, introduce another appropriate factor and you'll notice the insights begin to appear. Each additional factor, if applied properly, will give more insight, more revelation and more synergy.

That's X for multiply.

As you begin to progress towards your goal, introduce all twenty-six other factors and notice how this ups your chances. You cannot fail! Here are all twenty-six characteristics: notice their accumulative power. Be aware that we have not studied Y or Z yet. They come next...

A, attention
It all starts with attention. No progress will be made until you give the change that you want – whether physical ("I'd like a bigger house"), mental ("I'd like to be more creative") or career ("I'd like to be a breakfast show DJ") – sufficient attention. And by that we mean appropriate and dedicated time, energy and mindset.

B, belief
As we give attention we may find that we are not getting the progress we want, not because of a lack of technique, but because of the psychology of progress. Maybe we are being held back by a limiting belief. Beliefs drive our behaviour which drives our results. If we are not getting the results we want despite working hard on our behaviour, we can change our belief to the empowering one which gets us the results that we need.

C, compass

What are we giving attention to? To what we want, of course! How do we know what we want? Did we decide or did school condition us or consumer marketing set up a desire? A way to give it some excellent consideration is to study our LifeCompass℠. Our compass considers the important areas of our life to help us: career; mind/body; finance; relationships; fun; contribution.

D, decision

We will create the change by making a decision. However a decision is not a decision until we have taken an action. And actions themselves have distinct characteristics that ensure they are viable and work.

E, emotional intelligence

IQ is our pure numerical/linguistic ability. IQ is strongly genetic and although we can damage it (for example, with alcohol or drugs) we cannot significantly improve it. But we can improve our emotional intelligence, often known as EQ. And so much of what we wish to achieve will depend upon our ability to manage our moods and to liaise with others; this is EQ. EQ is twice as important as IQ, according to Daniel Goleman's research. As we create the changes we wish for, we will need our emotional intelligence as much as our numerical or linguistic intelligence.

F, fear

Fear may loom as we step out on the journey. But what is fear? Fear is not a hindrance, fear is a help. Feel the fear, get focused, prepare and do it anyway. Isolate your fears and turn them into allies.

G, Goal-Setting Formula

To get your success, start following a plan: the Goal-Setting Formula. Decide what you want; choose the best strategy available and go for it. And if it doesn't work, learn. Regroup and learn again.

H, hero

You'll have noticed that a lot of this stuff is tough. It's perhaps hard for you to do. You'll need a particularly resourceful state; you'll need to be a hero, an individual who does what is necessary, not for the glory, not for the prestige, but because it is necessary.

I, internally-referenced

Unfortunately not everyone in the world will be as supportive as you would like, so stay internally-referenced, rather than externally referenced. Do not ignore feedback, do not be selfish. But do acknowledge your own feelings and goals, your own principles and go for it.

J, journey

As you recognize these challenges along the way – that your strategy does not always work first time and that your friends are not all supportive of what you are doing – don't give up. Assuming, of course, it's what you still want. Simply accept feedback and comments, and adjust. That's where the true learning lies: on the journey, not the destination.

K, killer app

And when you get frustrated, begin to lose it, use your Killer App: JFDI. There are times when no more messing: Just F*c*ing Do It. Stop the intellectual and get practical.

L, lifelong learning

Be a lifelong learner. Those GCSEs, or college stuff or even that MBA: their sell-by date or usefulness expires very quickly. Become a lifelong learner. Become absolutely dedicated to becoming the best you can.

M, motivation

Motivation is not an accident. Do not wait until you are motivated; start and then you will become motivated.

N, niche

This is one of the fundamentals of the A to Z. Identify your niche, your specialist area. Then suddenly it will become a whole lot easier. Multiplying these characteristics in your niche is amazing.

O, organized

I know it seems a little dull – but everything will fall apart unless you can be organized. What are you going to focus on? Yes, of course that is critical, but how will you ensure that you do focus on it and keep it in your face?

P, passion

Passion. By now, if you have worked hard (did I mention that?), you will have found that your motivation and energy is beginning to build. That is, you are revealing the true you; you are working on what is important. You are becoming authentic! Authenticity builds passion. Passion builds authenticity.

Q, quantum leap

To get the breakthroughs you wish for, you need some quantum breakthroughs, you need to be radical – you need to make a quantum leap. Quantum leaps ignore intermediate sequential incremental steps; they just do it.

R, rainmaker

To get the changes to happen you will need to influence. This of course will depend upon the EQ skills that you have, on who you know, but also on your ability to make rain, to ensure that things happen, to sell.

S, success

This is it. You need to define it. You've done a lot of work now. But what is success for you? And hopefully you have left your preconceptions behind. Have you decided?

T, today

So what are you doing today? Are you still reading, being intellectual? Or are you actually doing anything? How about right now? Take a ten-minute break, decide half a dozen objectives and do them.

U, uncertainty

And recognize that it won't all be definite, be certain. Accept uncertainty. Be certain about it!

V, vision

And get your vision in your face. Your vision is your overall driver.

W, who

Work fully with your virtual team. Remember that there are a lot of people who can help you.

X

And multiply the benefits.

Y

And recognize the complementary forces.

Z

And recognize the changing nature of success. As you grow and develop, so will success.

Talent is in choices
ROBERT DE NIRO

Y is Yin and Yang

Yin +Yang

A strong theme, that you will no doubt have noticed during these writings, is: "To be successful you do have to fail."

Success is so often the implementation of complementary natures, such as success and failure. Rather than accepting one (as in "success is our only option: we will not tolerate any kind of failure") or judging (as in "don't show your emotions in negotiation") we begin to realise that they both have a role. It is so often the fuzziness in between two extremes, such as a bit of "masculine-think" and a bit of "feminine-think". It is so often achieving an in-between flow state, rather than a clearly defined state.

This is the Yin and Yang of success; the complementary states which make up the whole. Often our polarized thinking or conditioning has isolated just one of a complementary pair, such as
   success in success/failure, or
   certainty in certain/uncertain or
   masculine in masculine/feminine.

But if we do work in that way our picture of the world is incomplete. We have seen how we cannot have success without failure. As our learning develops, we realise that there are many other complementary pairs of which we have only considered one aspect. So much science, for instance, has been dependent upon initial intuition. And how do we get certainty without exploring uncertainty?

As I coached Lucy, a clear challenge to her vision became apparent at every turn; she really didn't like discomfort. Now we're not talking about being homeless, or ill, or stressed, but about discomfort; a word I choose carefully.

Lucy wanted to move from Sales into Marketing. She is a successful salesperson, earning a high salary with a nice car and a lot of prestige. But she wanted a change and to do less travelling: she favoured marketing. Certainly career diagnostics suggested that this would be a good move for her.

But as I mentioned, there was a challenge; she didn't want any discomfort. What was the discomfort she feared? That she'd lower her overall earnings, take a more junior position for a while. And there was the possibility of failure.

A discussion on Yin and Yang was helpful. She began to understand that to achieve greater comfort eventually, you might have to experience some discomfort. To get success, you have to risk failure. In fact for any desirable state, you might well have to experience the flipside. To value any quality (such as true love or happiness) you may well need to experience the exact opposite.

Lucy made the change. She coped with the discomfort. But more importantly she learnt something that would be important all through her life.

Here are some more complementary states to consider.

Certainty/uncertainty

We have just looked at this in U for Uncertainty. Certainty is not necessarily better than uncertainty. We will see that this true of all the complementary pairs we will study (and, of course, the ones we will not study here, either). Don't "choose one". Yes, you will have a preference, but practice developing the least preferred. In these notes I will emphasize the one that often needs more attention.

Comfort/discomfort

When we strive we tend to look for something better, something more comfortable. But to get to that point we have to go through considerable discomfort. Be careful of avoiding discomfort. Often, a higher more exciting level is achieved via a period of discomfort. Step on, step up.

Today/tomorrow

Tomorrow often seems the perfect time scale for getting things done, as in "Great, I think I'll do that tomorrow." However, without action today, nothing ever will be achieved. Learn to flex your time scales.

On the other hand, today is sometimes too intense, too here. We need to let go, accept what didn't go so well today and return tomorrow. Incubate for a while, and then it will be a whole lot clearer.

Science/intuition

Wow! What a method, the scientific method: logical, analytical, didactic. From Descartes to Newton. Collect your data, test it. Apply appropriate scientific methodology. Only then might you draw a conclusion. This is driven into us in school, and in business, too.

Then we feel guilty if we simply "feel" the solution. We know it's right, and so often it is. And ironically, so have many scientists who "knew" first and rationalized later. Allow yourself some intuition.

Success/failure

To be successful we must have needed to learn. That learning must have required us to fail along the way. Success is therefore often associated with failure. It has been said that if you are not failing then perhaps you are not trying hard enough.

Masculine/feminine

There are times when the "traditional" masculine attributes are very helpful and powerful. There are many times when the feminine attributes are what we need. This is not a sexist comment. We all recognize what we mean by more masculine and more feminine approaches. And we all know that they both have their strengths and weaknesses in a particular situation. The important thing is not to generalize from masculine and feminine attributes to male and female, the sexes. Secondly, recognize when one is a particular asset: feminine characteristics such as listening and empathy are excellent in selling; masculine ones, such as bias to action, can be invaluable in, say, project management.

Journey/destination

To have a goal, a destination is vital. But do not get overly hung up about this goal. Once you have it, concentrate on the journey. The destination gives the journey meaning, but the journey is where we get the pleasure, the understanding and the learning.

Easy/hard

The easy bit will come when we have done the hard bits. However as soon as you have done some easy bits there will be some more hard bits. Simply have an easy expectation of both parts: don't get frustrated when it's no longer "easy".

Progress/regress

Success will often seem three steps forward and two steps backward. That's because it is. When we have consolidated one part, that exposes the weakness in another.

Knowing/doubting

At times you will be very confident that what you are doing is absolutely the right thing to do. Then you may have doubts, sometimes dreadful doubts. How can I have been so sure about this project, this relationship? Recognize that doubt will help build your knowing at a later stage. Allow knowing/doubting to sit alongside each other.

Wealth/poverty

We appreciate wealth when we have had poverty. And when we are wealthy we can appreciate simplicity, or poverty. Certainly we are not condoning the terrible poverty which many people in the world have to endure. What I am talking about here is the ability to relinquish possessions, which ironically can give us the freedom to think and act.

Young/old

Why such a fuss about the label "young or old"? We have three ways of registering our age (at least). Chronological is that dictated by your birth certificate. Physiological is dictated by biological indicators such as blood pressure, skin elasticity, etc. And your psychological age is how young or old you feel. That's the key. Choose your age. Sometimes you want the vigour of youth; at other times the wisdom of age. You choose.

Simple/complicated

Too often we feel that for something to be useful it must be complicated. How about if we began to value simplicity? Not simplistic, but simplicity. Listen to the jargon put forward in business: "leverage the business model". What an earth do they mean?

Abundant/restricted

Abundant thinkers realise that by working together they can increase the size of the pie. Restricted thinkers are made anxious by that idea. They only want to take a bigger slice of the pie. Of course restricted thinkers get absolutely focused.

For those of us who already consider ourselves achievers, this unreliability of state can be very disconcerting. True success comes in recognizing that to truly empower a certain state, the other side must be fully understood. We only really truly understand the state of focus when we have been defocused for a while.

So, to use these characteristics:

1. Remember that every state has a benefit, even those ones which initially seem less attractive. If you are feeling down, firstly ask, "How can I use this state?" And then quickly and appropriately change the state. Some states may seem more pleasant than others, but if we genuinely think, "I need this state," it's going to give us value and we can learn to enjoy it.

2. States are complementary. We need one state to illustrate the importance of the other.

3. State is a function of mindset. Once we have got what we need from a state (e.g., a state of lethargy might be a reminder that we really need to look after our health more), then by changing our focus we can change our state.

4. State is a function of physiology. Again, once we have gained what we can from a state, we can think what would be a resourceful physiology: simply to sit up straight, perhaps?

5. State is a function of language. Always choose your language. If you insist on talking in a less than resourceful way, then you won't feel particularly resourceful.

6. Taking Action. When you are in a state which you don't want, think, "Is this the complementary side of a state which I do want? How is it helping me?"

When you are in a state you want but don't seem to be getting the result you want, decide whether there are any other complementary states to which you can get access.

Z

Z is Zen and the Art of being Successful

Zen

Success is undoubtedly a little paradoxical: a moving target. As youngsters we often seek a role: to be a footballer, or a hairdresser, or a vet, or a rock star or a teacher. Once we have a role (and, of course, it is rarely the one we initially desired) we then seek stuff: a house, a bigger house. A car, a bigger car. A kettle, an espresso machine. Our desire is constantly shifting and appears to be ever upgrading. With each new role or acquisition, our desire steps up a notch. Sometimes, when we stop and reflect, we wonder what we are chasing. What does it take to be happy? Especially as when we get bigger roles and more stuff we sometimes seem to become less happy and gain more worries!

And then one day it dawns on us that we crave some simple things such as time to ourselves, or an unpressurized game of tennis or an hour just to read (and not email). Or a theatre trip, or time developing a relationship. And then the ultimate quest becomes some "time to be" as we realise that we have truly reached the far side of complexity: the wisdom of success. The wisdom of success is that true success is just a few simple qualities: time to be, time with and for others, leaving a legacy, simple things done well, a walk, laughter... Success itself is not at all complicated. We're very good at making it so. For many this is an "aha" moment. To be successful we don't need a particular role, nor a grand job title, nor do we need to acquire a range of stuff. We just need to be; to enjoy what is there anyway.

Many of us are in danger of accelerating away rapidly from what we truly want.

It is in the nature of humans to grow. But perhaps we have been seduced by the pressures of society and by the marketers (and we are all involved) into thinking it is more complicated than it really is.

It was a problem many people would have loved to have had: Jack had more than enough in the bank, a couple of fast cars and a hell of a job title with the salary to go with it. But he felt it was not what he wanted.

"Ever since I was a teenager I've chased 'stuff' and roles," he said. "I wanted to work at the right company and I wanted the right job title. And then we had to live in the right house in the right area. And then we wanted to get the kids into the right school. And you know, now we're there, now by most people's estimation we've made it, I don't really want any of it: I don't feel happy and I don't feel satisfied. I really must admit that I thought it would bring security – which it hasn't: I worry more than ever. I really don't think the kids appreciate any of the stuff they have, and we haven't had the time to build a close relationship with them."

Jack was certainly suffering – Zen and the Art of Success. He had found that success is a constantly moving target that tends to shift from the more tangible to the less tangible. And perhaps we have to go through that learning before we truly appreciate what success is for us.

The answer to the question "Will we ever be really happy?" is, of course, yes. When we decide to be happy. Happy is something we can be and it need not be attached to a role or a thing. This is not being silly. Of course a beautiful sunset can be inspirational. The right person can bring special joy into our life and... But do not wait for the beautiful sunset, or expect relationships always to be easy.

Our goal, ultimately, is not to attach success overly to a role or thing. Our health is so good that we feel great anyway and can cope with the everyday knocks of life. We are not worried by our job title – we are simply there to do the best job that we can. Imagine how much more relaxing and easier this state can be; simply choose it.

To be happy, decide to be happy. Choose to see the best in any situation; focus on what is going well, look after your mind/body, develop your relationships. Realise that happiness consists of the fundamentals such as freedom and the ability to grow. You will have no doubt heard that great quote: "No one on their deathbed ever said 'I should have spent more time at the office'."

It may help to remember to focus more on the journey and less on the destination, focus on the process more than the goal. And to remember that it won't always be easy. Sometimes it will be very hard. And then it may well be easy for a while.

And just when you thought you knew what success was, it will change. And that's OK!

Zen and the Art of Being Successful. Let's take a deeper look at each word.

Zen

As in do less, achieve more: stop running and micro-scheduling. Stop relying on your defensiveness. Slow down, use your reflective intelligence and a whole lot more. Tune into your intuition. Settle into compass time. Be aware of that flow state: a state in which you are not trying but everything has come together for you. You have endless energy. You are enjoying what you are doing. Zen, as in accept apparent paradoxes such as more is less and less is more. And soft is hard and hard is soft. So much of what we learn in school, college and corporate life is so far from the real wisdom of true effectiveness, of true success. Thus soft skills make the difference (hence soft is hard) but so often they are ignored because they are not measurable. Or more money is better. No. Not necessarily. Because more money often comes from longer hours. And with longer hours you don't get any chance to enjoy it anyway.

Art
Success is certainly part science. We have already seen, for example, the Goal-Seeking Formula. But in addition to this we need to think about the art of success. Those more non-measurable, qualitative aspects such as:

- **Intuition**: sometimes something just feels that it is right; sometimes you just know. Remember the scientific model is just one model, one point of view. Don't ignore intuition simply because it doesn't seem to have the full seal of approval, especially from many in the business and scientific communities. Many, many people use intuition; they then often "backward rationalize" with science.

- **Synchronicity**: once you start using your intuition fully and noticing your progress, you'll start to notice interesting patterns. Some may be quite marvellous such as the right people being available at the right times to support you. Or maybe, more ordinarily, you keep noting an article that is so appropriate for you at the time. These meaningful occurrences are a higher intuition. They are synchronicity.

- **Flow**: A state described so well by Mihaly Csikszentmihalyi in his book *Flow: The Classical Work on How to Achieve Happiness.* It's all happening easily. That's flow.

Being

This is when it becomes wired-in. Doing is always harder work. And having is only on the route.

Successful

You are successful. Now you have some great ideas on how to be even more so. If you are wondering how to start and what to do next, simply take one letter at a time per day over the next month. Or when you awake, choose a letter. Any letter which comes to mind and focus on that.

So to capitalize on the Zen-like features of success:

1. **Start the Journey.** Be fearless at this point; it's all learning anyway. You won't know whether it is "correct" when you start. And equally you won't know until you start. Boldly ask for the new position. Boldly submit your manuscript. Boldly start the fitness regime. Be greater than your reluctance. Be greater than your ego, greater even than your addiction to staying in bed in the morning. Set yourself an exciting new standard, where you take action on a project by starting.

2. **Learn as you go.** Remember to let go of that certainty which you crave. You will not get it as you grow and develop. Just when you have got it, it will slip away again. If you don't get the promotion or don't get the part you had wanted, stay resourceful. What can you learn from that situation? With hindsight what would you have done differently? Now that you realise that route doesn't work what would be a better one?

Revisit U for Uncertainty. Remember as we allow uncertainly into our lives new, interesting connections appear.

3. Love the challenges. Who said it was meant to be easy? Many of us live in a world where comfort has become our measure of success. Be willing to cope with short-term discomfort in order to get to where you want to be.

Realise that every challenge is a step significantly closer to your goal. The biggest setbacks are potentially the biggest breakthroughs. Remember how you feel when you've achieved something in spite of enormous obstacles.

Each little bit of discomfort we get used to coping with expands our comfort zone. Now we can get up earlier, study for longer, handle our manager better.

4. Stay focused. Keep it in your face. Never let a day go by where you don't focus on what it is you wish to achieve. Be creative; stick it on the fridge. In the fridge? On the wall? On the shaving mirror? In your make-up bag? As part of your screen saver? In the car?

Have that longer-term vision: promotion, better work/life balance, your own business, being a writer, an artist. And go for it.

5. Stay light-hearted. Sure, it's going to be stressful at times. Your best antidote is great humour. Enlightened: the ability to "lighten up". Whatever you do, have fun. What are some ridiculous ways you can keep it in your face? What are some daft comments for those who put down your exploits?

6. Be curious about paradox. Be intensely interested in what goes well and what goes less well. They are simply the two sides of progress. Paradoxically it appears that the two sides go together (perhaps revisit Y for Yin and Yang).

> Failure/success
> Masculine/feminine
> Structure/flow
> Journey/destination

7. Support others on the route. It will help them, but it will – without doubt – help you. Have you noticed how you understand things much better when you teach them? That kindness, that "going out," will undoubtedly be rewarded. But maybe not immediately. And maybe not in a similar format. And, interestingly, maybe not even from the person who gave it. But it will be returned.

8. Never, ever give up on your version of success. You grow and develop, just when you have got it.

Journey not
Destination

Journey

Where to next? Well, as you realise (letter J), we've certainly not finished. This book has got you onto the path and you may want to take a look at www.strategicedge.co.uk for some further inspiration and certainly for further reading. The website will also have details of my workshops and I do hope you will attend one of those at some stage.

Take a decision: get started if you haven't already.

Remember the quote from Goethe?

Whatever you can do, or dream you can, begin it! Boldness has genius, magic and power in it. Begin it now.
GOETHE.